Scenes from
a Marriage

Ingmar Bergman

SCENES
FROM A
MARRIAGE

Translated from the Swedish by Alan Blair

PANTHEON BOOKS
A Division of Random House, New York

FIRST AMERICAN EDITION

English Translation Copyright © 1974 by Alan Blair.

Library of Congress Cataloging in Publication Data

Bergman, Ingmar, 1918–
Scenes from a Marriage.

Translation of *Scener ur ett äktenskap*.
I. Title.
PT9875.B533S313   839.7'2'74   74–4753
ISBN 0-394-49305-2

The photographs throughout this book were taken by
Lars Karlsson. Since they are of the Swedish television film
based on this text, slight details may vary.

PREFACE

To prevent the constrained reader from getting lost in the text I have decided—contrary to my habit—to write a commentary on the six scenes. Those who are offended by such guidance should skip the following lines.

First scene: Johan and Marianne are conventional and set in their ways and believe in material security. They have never found their middle-class way of life oppressive or false. They have conformed to a pattern which they are prepared to pass on. Their former political activity is a confirmation of this rather than a contradiction.

In the first scene they present a pretty picture of an almost ideal marriage, which is confronted moreover with an inferno-like relationship. They are smug in a quiet way, convinced that they have arranged everything for the best. The air is thick with makeshift solutions and well-meant platitudes. Peter and Katarina appear as lunatics to be pitied, while Johan and Marianne have arranged for the best in this best of worlds. All the same, at the end of this scene they receive a slight setback. They are faced with a choice. A sore, apparently trifling, breaks open, heals, and forms a scar, but under the scar an infection has formed. That's my idea anyway. If someone else wishes to think differently, that's fine.

Second scene: Everything is still ideal, almost splendid. Small worries are solved in joking agreement. Their professions and working environments are presented. Marianne is aware of a vague anxiety. She can't define it, still less pin it down, but instinctively she feels that something is wrong between her and Johan. She makes a lame and not very successful effort to repair the dimly sensed rift. Johan has several mysterious telephone calls. One evening when they've been to the theater and seen *A Doll's House* (what else would they have seen?), there is a sudden feeling of discord between them; they try to make light of it and finally sweep it under the rug.

Third scene: The blow falls. In rather a brutal way Johan announces that he is in love with another woman and is going to leave. He is full of vital eagerness to act and oxidized by the cheerful selfishness of the new infatuation. Marianne is thunderstruck. Utterly defenseless. Totally unprepared. Within a few minutes she changes in front of our eyes into a bleeding and trembling sore. Humiliation and perplexity.

Fourth scene: They meet again after quite a long time. Things have started to go wrong for Johan, though it is not noticeable. On the contrary. As for Marianne, there are signs of recovery, though they are extremely vague and are mixed up with the past: her ties to Johan, the ulcerous loneliness, the longing for everything to be as it was before. Their encounter is painful and clumsy in its mixture of reconciliation and aggressiveness. For brief moments they reach one another through isolation and aloofness. Everything is fragile, infected, ragged. This is a very sad scene.

Fifth scene: Now there is a terrible blowup. Marianne is finding her feet again and Johan is losing his grip on reality. They have the bright idea of starting divorce proceedings together and of engaging the same lawyer. One evening in early summer they meet at Johan's office to sign the divorce papers. Suddenly everything explodes and they give vent to all the aggressions, all the hate, all the mutual boredom and rage that they have been suppressing for years. Bit by bit they are dehumanized and at last they become really nasty and behave like maniacs who have only one thought in their minds: to maul each other physically and mentally. In these efforts they are even a degree worse than Peter and Katarina in the first scene, who have a certain routine in their inferno and are, as it were, more professional in their savagery. Johan and Marianne have not yet learned this extreme restraint. In short, they want to destroy one another, and they very nearly succeed.

Sixth scene: My idea now is that two new people begin to emerge from all this devastation. Maybe that is a little too optimistic but I can't help it, that's how it turned out. Both Johan and Marianne have walked through the vale of tears and made it rich in springs. They are beginning to acquire a new knowledge of themselves, in a manner of speaking. This is not just a matter of resignation, but concerns love too. For the first time, Marianne sits down and listens to her troublesome mother. Johan looks at his own situation with forgiveness and is good to Marianne in a new and adult way. Everything is still in confusion and nothing is any better. All relations are muddled and their lives are incontestably based on a heap of wretched compromises. But somehow they are now citizens of the world of reality in quite a different way from before. At least I think so. There's no solution at hand, anyway, so there's no happy ending. Nice as it would have been to arrive at one. If for no other reason, to annoy all artistically sensitive people, who, disgusted by this quite understandable work, will be aesthetically sick after the very first scene.

What more is there to say? This opus took three months to write, but rather a long part of my life to experience. I'm not sure that it would have turned out better had it been the other way round, though it would have seemed nicer. I have felt a kind of affection for these people while I've been occupied with them. They have grown rather contradictory, sometimes anxiously childish, sometimes pretty grown-up. They talk quite a lot of rubbish, now and then saying something sensible. They are nervous, happy, selfish, stupid, kind, wise, self-sacrificing, affectionate, angry, gentle, sentimental, insufferable, and lovable. All jumbled up. Now let's see what happens.

I.B.

Fårö, May 1972

FIRST SCENE
Innocence and Panic

CHARACTERS

JOHAN

MARIANNE

KARIN and EVA, their daughters

MRS. PALM, the interviewer

PHOTOGRAPHER

PETER

KATARINA

I

MARIANNE *and* JOHAN *are being interviewed in their home. They are sitting, rather stiffly and on their best behavior, beside each other on a sofa. Quite a sofa, at that. It's round and curved and Victorian and upholstered in green; it has friendly arms, soft cushions, and carved legs; it is a monstrosity of coziness. A handsome oil lamp can be glimpsed on a table. The background consists of massive bookshelves. On another table are tea, toast and jam, and sherry. The interviewer,* MRS. PALM, *is sitting with her back to the camera. She has set up a small tape recorder among the plates and cups. A bearded photographer moves about the room, popping up and disappearing.*

MRS. PALM *(Gaily)* We always begin with a standard question. To get over the first nervousness.

JOHAN I'm not particularly nervous.

MARIANNE Nor am I.

MRS. PALM *(Still more gaily)* All the better. The question is: How would you describe yourselves in a few words?

JOHAN That's not an easy one.

MRS. PALM Not so difficult either, surely?

JOHAN I mean, there's risk of a misunderstanding.

MRS. PALM   Do you think so?

JOHAN   Yes. It might sound conceited if I described myself as extremely intelligent, successful, youthful, well-balanced, and sexy. A man with a world conscience, cultivated, well-read, popular, and a good mixer. Let me see, what else can I think of . . . friendly. Friendly in a nice way even to people who are worse off. I like sports. I'm a good family man. A good son. I have no debts and I pay my taxes. I respect our government whatever it does, and I love our royal family. I've left the state church. Is this enough or do you want more details? I'm a splendid lover. Aren't I, Marianne?

MRS. PALM   *(With a smile)*   Perhaps we can return to the question. How about you, Marianne? What do you have to say?

MARIANNE   Hmm, what can I say . . . I'm married to Johan and have two daughters.

MRS. PALM   Yes . . .

MARIANNE   That's all I can think of for the moment.

MRS. PALM   There must be something . . .

MARIANNE   I think Johan is rather nice.

JOHAN   Kind of you, I'm sure.

MARIANNE   We've been married for ten years.

JOHAN   I've just renewed the contract.

MARIANNE   I doubt if I have the same natural appreciation of my own excellence as Johan. But to tell the truth, I'm glad I can live the life I do. It's a good life, if you know what I mean. Well, what else can I say . . . Oh dear, this is difficult!

JOHAN   She has a nice figure.

MARIANNE   You're joking. I'm trying to take this thing seriously. I have two daughters, Karin and Eva.

JOHAN   You've already said that.

MRS. PALM *(Giving up)*   Perhaps we can take up the question again later. By the way! What about a picture with your daughters? Here on the sofa with mother and father?

MARIANNE   They'll be home from school soon.

MRS. PALM   Oh, good. Well, let's start with a few facts. I'd like to know your ages.

JOHAN   I'm forty-two. But you wouldn't think so to look at me, would you?

MARIANNE   I'm thirty-five.

JOHAN   Both of us come from almost indecently middle-class homes.

MARIANNE   Johan's father is a doctor.

JOHAN   And my mother's the motherly type. Very much so.

MARIANNE   My father's a lawyer. It was decided from the outset that I was to be a lawyer too. I'm the youngest of seven children. Mother ran a big household. Nowadays she takes it easier.

JOHAN   She does?
(Polite smiles)

MARIANNE   The funny thing about us both is that we actually get along very well with our parents. We see quite a lot of each other. There has never been any friction to speak of.

MRS. PALM   Perhaps we'd better say something about your professions.

JOHAN   I'm an associate professor at the Psychotechnical Institute.

MARIANNE   I specialized in family law and am employed by a law firm. Most of my work has to do with divorces and so on. The interesting thing is that the whole time you're brought into contact with—

PHOTOGRAPHER   *(Popping up)* Will you look at each other, please. Like that, hold it . . . I just want to . . . Sorry . . .

MARIANNE   It's awful, I feel like such a fool.

MRS. PALM   Only at first. How did you meet?

MARIANNE   Let Johan tell you.

JOHAN   Good Lord, *that's* interesting!

MARIANNE   At any rate, it wasn't love at first sight.

JOHAN   Both of us had a large circle of friends and we used to meet at all sorts of parties. Also, we were politically active for several years and we went in for amateur dramatics quite a lot as students. But I can't say we made any very deep impression on each other. Marianne thought I was stuck-up.

MARIANNE   He was having a much-discussed affair with a pop singer and that gave him a certain image and made him insufferable.

JOHAN   And Marianne was nineteen and married to a fool, whose only saving grace was that he was the apple of his rich father's eye.

MARIANNE   But he was awfully kind. And I was madly in love.

Besides, I got pregnant almost at once. And that also meant something.

MRS. PALM   But how was it that . . .

JOHAN   That we two came together? That was Marianne's idea, actually.

MARIANNE   My child died soon after it was born and then my husband and I got a divorce, rather to our relief. Johan had been dropped by that pop singer and was a little less stuck-up. We were feeling a bit lonely and tousled. So I suggested trying to make a go of it. We were not in the least in love with one another, we were just miserable.

JOHAN   We got along very well together and really got down to our studies.

MARIANNE   So we started living together. Our mothers never batted an eye, though we thought they'd be terribly shocked. Not at all! In fact, they became good friends. Suddenly we were accepted as Johan and Marianne. After six months we got married.

JOHAN   Besides, by then we were in love.

MARIANNE   Terribly.

JOHAN   We were considered an ideal married couple.

MARIANNE   And so it has gone on.

MRS. PALM   No complications?

MARIANNE   We've had no material worries. We're on good terms with friends and relations on both sides. We have good jobs that we like. We're healthy.

JOHAN   And so on and so on, to an almost vulgar degree. Security, order, comfort, and loyalty. It all has a suspiciously successful look.

MARIANNE   Naturally, like other people, we have our differences. That goes without saying. But we agree on all the important things.

MRS. PALM   Don't you ever quarrel?

JOHAN   Oh yes, Marianne does.

MARIANNE   Johan is very slow to anger, so it calms me down.

MRS. PALM   It sounds fantastic. The whole thing.

MARIANNE   Someone was saying to us just last night that the very lack of problems is in itself a serious problem. I suspect it's true. A life like ours always has its dangers. We're well aware of that.

JOHAN   The world is going to the devil and I claim the right to mind my own business. Every political system is corrupt. It makes me sick to think of these new salvation gospels. Whoever controls the computers will win the game. I hold the unpopular view of live and let live.

MARIANNE   I don't agree with Johan.

MRS. PALM   Oh, what do you think then?

MARIANNE   I believe in fellow-feeling.

MRS. PALM   What do you mean by that?

MARIANNE   If everyone learned to care about each other right from childhood, the world would be a different place, I'm certain of that.

PHOTOGRAPHER   Don't move! Keep that expression. That's it. Thank you.

MARIANNE   Here are Karin and Eva. I'll tell them to tidy themselves.
(MARIANNE *hurries out and is heard talking to her daughters.* JOHAN *fills his pipe and exchanges a rather uncertain but polite smile with the interviewer, who sips her cold tea and is at a momentary loss for a question*)

JOHAN   To tell you the truth, it's not such a simple matter.

MRS. PALM   What do you mean?

JOHAN   We used to think that nothing could happen to us. Now we know better. That's the only difference.

MRS. PALM   Are you afraid of the future?

JOHAN   If I stopped to think I'd be petrified with fear. Or so I imagine. So I don't think. I'm fond of this cozy old sofa and that oil lamp. They give me an illusion of security which is so fragile that it's almost comic. I like Bach's "St. Matthew Passion" though I'm not religious, because it gives me feelings of piety and belonging. Our families see a lot of each other and I depend very much on this contact, as it reminds me of my childhood when I felt I was protected. I like what Marianne said about fellow-feeling. It's good for a conscience which worries on quite the wrong occasions. I think you must have a kind of technique to be able to live and be content with your life. In fact, you have to practice quite hard not giving a damn about anything. The people I admire most are those who can take life as a joke. I can't. I have too little sense of humor for a feat like that. You won't print this, will you?

MRS. PALM   No, I'm afraid it's a little too complicated for our women readers. If you forgive my saying so.
(*Pause*)

JOHAN   What shall we talk about now?

MRS. PALM   Oh, I have lots of questions. (MARIANNE *comes in and sits down on the sofa with her daughters,* EVA, *12, and* KARIN, *11. They're a little stiff, giggly, embarrassed, and delighted, combed and dressed to have their picture taken. Mutual how-do-you-dos. Grouping and regrouping conducted by the photographer.* JOHAN *clutches his pipe. When the picture of the family group has been taken the children are allowed to disappear into the kitchen and have their afternoon cup of cocoa and cheese sandwich.* JOHAN *excuses himself, saying that he must make a phone call, and vanishes, more quickly than politely.* MRS. PALM *seizes the opportunity. After all, it* is *a woman's magazine)* I don't think you and I have met since our school days.

MARIANNE   Do you often see our old schoolmates?

MRS. PALM   Actually I don't. (*Going right to the point*) I gather that you and Johan have a good life together. Haven't you? I mean, you're really happy. Aren't you? Everything you tell me sounds simply marvelous. But then why shouldn't some people be granted perfection.

MARIANNE   I don't know that we've got perfection. But we do have a good life. I mean, we're happy. Oh yes, we're happy.

MRS. PALM (*Seizing on this*)   How would you define the word happiness?

MARIANNE   Must I really?

MRS. PALM (*Gravely*)   This is a woman's magazine, Marianne.

MARIANNE   If I thought up something to say about happiness, Johan would only laugh at me. No, I can't. You must hit on something yourself.

MRS. PALM (*Roguishly*)   Don't try to wriggle out of it now.

MARIANNE   I suppose happiness is being content. I don't long for anything. Except for the summer, of course. *(Pause)* I wish it could always be like this. That nothing ever changed.

MRS. PALM   *(Her appetite whetted)* What do you have to say about fidelity?

MARIANNE   Well, really!

MRS. PALM   You must help me put some body into this. Johan's awfully sweet, but I didn't get much out of him.

MARIANNE   Fidelity?

MRS. PALM   Yes, fidelity. Between man and woman. Of course.

MARIANNE   Fidelity. Hmm, what can one say about that . . .

MRS. PALM   In your profession you must surely have come across—

MARIANNE   I wonder if fidelity can exist other than as a matter of course. I don't think fidelity can ever be a compulsion or a resolution. You can never promise anyone fidelity. Either it's there or it isn't. I like to be faithful to Johan, therefore I am faithful. But naturally I don't know how it will be tomorrow or next week.

MRS. PALM   Have you always been faithful to Johan?

MARIANNE   *(Coldly)*   Now I think we're getting *too* personal.

MRS. PALM   Forgive me. Now I have only one last question, while Johan is on the phone. What do you have to say about love? You *must* say something about love. It's part of this series to give your views on love.

MARIANNE   And if I don't want to?

MRS. PALM   Then I'll have to make up something myself and it won't be half as good.

MARIANNE   No one has told me what love is. And I'm not even sure it's necessary to know. But if you want a detailed description, you can look in the Bible—Paul told us what love is. The trouble is, his definition squashes us flat. If love is what Paul says it is, then it's so rare that hardly anyone has known it. But as a set piece to be read out at weddings and other solemn occasions, those verses are rather impressive. I think it's enough if you're kind to the person you're living with. Affection is also a good thing. Comradeship and tolerance and a sense of humor. Moderate ambitions for one another. If you can supply those ingredients, then . . . then love's not so important.

MRS. PALM   Why are you so upset?

MARIANNE   In my profession I'm dealing the whole time with people who have collapsed under impossible demands for emotional expression. It's barbarous. I wish that . . .

MRS. PALM   What do you wish?

MARIANNE   I don't know. I can't see through this problem, so I'd rather not talk about it. But I wish that people . . . that we were not forced to play a lot of parts we don't want to play. That we could be simpler and gentler with each other. Don't you think so too?

MRS. PALM *(Alert)*   That life could be a little more romantic!

MARIANNE   No, I didn't mean that actually. In fact, I meant just the opposite. You see how badly I express myself. Can't we talk about food and children instead? It's something a bit more concrete, anyway.

MRS. PALM   Perhaps we did digress.

MARIANNE   Yes, I think we did.
   (Polite smile)

MRS. PALM   Well, how do you manage both job and home?

———

JOHAN *and* MARIANNE *have asked* PETER *and* KATARINA *to dinner. Their daughters do the serving. Spirits are high.* JOHAN *is reading aloud from a woman's magazine.*

JOHAN *(Reading aloud)*   "Marianne has folksong-blue eyes that seem to light up from within. When I ask her how she manages both job and home she gives a little introspective smile as though she were keeping a sweet secret and answers rather evasively that she copes all right, that she and Johan help each other. 'It's a question of *mutual understanding,*' she says suddenly, brightening as Johan comes in and sits down beside her on the handsome heirloom sofa. He puts a protective arm around her shoulders and she snuggles up to him with a smile of security and trust. So I leave them, and I can't help noticing that they are secretly pleased when I go, so that they can once more be alone together. Two young people, strong, happy, with a constructive attitude toward life in general, but who have never forgotten all the same to give love first place."
   (As JOHAN *finishes reading there is spontaneous applause. Then they take another helping from the casserole and pour out more wine)*

MARIANNE   We regretted it and nearly died when we read the masterpiece, and wanted to change it all, but the editor said it was too late, unfortunately. There had been some mistake and the article had already gone to press.

JOHAN   We thought seriously of complaining to the authorities, but our mothers and daughters thought it was all wonderful, so we let it go. What chiefly riled me was that it said nothing about *my* eyes. Katarina! Take a look! Can't you see any secret glow in my eyes?

KATARINA   They look more like pools of darkness to me. Awfully sexy, actually.

PETER   Katarina has fallen hard for you of late.

KATARINA   Will you elope with me, Johan?

MARIANNE   I think a change would do Johan good. He's been so awfully conjugal for ten years now and never been unfaithful.

PETER   Are you so sure?

MARIANNE   I made up my mind at the outset to believe everything he said. Didn't I, Johan?

PETER   There, you see, Katarina?

KATARINA   Yes, but I'm sure Johan lies much more cleverly than you do, my silly old darling.

JOHAN   I'm afraid I have no imagination.

PETER   That's just the point. People with no imagination tell better lies than those with too much.

KATARINA   Peter dolls up his stories with far too many details. Sometimes I'm really touched.

MARIANNE   By the way, I read Peter's article in the *Technical Magazine.* Even I understood what it was about.

PETER   It was Katarina who wrote it.

JOHAN   Are you so clever, Katarina?

PETER   I was in Germany when they called up, so Katarina sat down then and there and wrote the article, and read it to me on the phone.

MARIANNE   But why does it say it's your article when Katarina wrote it?

KATARINA   It's not an instance of keeping women in their place. We always work together, you know.

JOHAN   How I envy you.

PETER   You wouldn't say that if you knew what goes on between us. To be honest, things are goddamn lousy right now. Skoal, Katarina. It doesn't matter my saying that when we're with Johan and Marianne, does it?

MARIANNE   What is it; Katarina?

KATARINA   Nothing. Nothing at all. It's just that I think Peter's so damned clumsy sometimes.

PETER   *Clumsy* was the word. I take a pride in being clumsy. And imaginative. I'm an all-round stinker, in fact, but I really can't help that.

JOHAN   Well, let's enjoy ourselves and not go into life's injustices.

PETER   No, we musn't forget—bearing in mind the recent magazine interview—that we're, so to speak, under a happy roof and are not to make any emotional stains. Skoal, Marianne. Even if I don't envy you your domestic bliss, I wish I had your skill with food—you're a marvelous cook.

MARIANNE   Katarina's much better than I am.

KATARINA   The trouble is, Peter thinks I poison the food.

PETER It's a standing joke in our house.

KATARINA You do understand it's a joke, don't you?

PETER A pretty sick one, if you ask me.

JOHAN *(Changing the subject)* Shall we go into the living-room? There's coffee and cake for dessert.

MARIANNE No, Katarina, please don't bother. The girls will clear the dishes and wash up. I've bribed them, you see. They like earning money. They're saving up for their summer vacation.

JOHAN Would you like a cigar, Peter? I have some rather special ones.

PETER No, thanks. I've given up smoking.

JOHAN You don't say! Congratulations!

KATARINA It has played such havoc with his nerves that I've begged him to start again. But now he won't smoke, just to annoy me. I can't stop, I've given up trying. I'll become as wrinkled as a mummy and I'll die of cancer, but never mind. Marianne dear, do you have an aspirin? I've had the most ghastly headache all day. No, I'll come with you. Then the boys can sit and exchange dirty stories in peace. (MARIANNE *and* KATARINA *go off to the bathroom, which is very elegant with marble and gilded taps, lots of mirrors, two sinks, and every imaginable luxury.* KATARINA *sits on the edge of the tub)* I only wanted to get away. I felt myself getting tipsy and then I'm awfully irritable. Poor Peter. It makes him feel like a cornered rat and he starts talking officialese and rolling his eyes.

MARIANNE You can lie on the bed for a while if you like.

KATARINA   No, it's all right. It's so quiet and peaceful here. You're kind, Marianne.

MARIANNE   You both seem to be going through a bad stretch just now.

KATARINA *(With a laugh)*   Yes, you could call it that.

MARIANNE   Why don't you separate for a while?

KATARINA   On the contrary, Marianne. We're going abroad on a long business trip. Our whole livelihood is based on our sticking together. We have everything together, you see. Peter has made over everything to me, and our business in

Italy depends entirely on what we do together. Then there are all these new synthetic materials that keep coming along and that we have to test. And I have to adjust my color schemes and patterns and Peter's so brilliant with his analyses. The whole lot would collapse if we split up. We just can't afford to.

MARIANNE Then can't you work together and live your own private lives?

KATARINA Do you think we haven't tried? You know that.

MARIANNE Yes, that's true.

KATARINA Peter says he's impotent with other women. I don't know whether he's lying, but I think he's telling the truth on that point. He goes nearly crazy if I refuse him. And the funny thing is that he's such a tender and expert lover. I quite enjoy having sex with him. Provided, of course, I have someone else.

MARIANNE Then you don't now?

KATARINA No. I've finished it off.

MARIANNE You poor thing.

KATARINA Jan couldn't cope with leading a double life. And leading a double life is the only thing I *can* cope with. So now all hell's broke loose, you see. Sometimes I hate Peter so much that I could torture him to death. When I can't sleep I lie thinking up the most extraordinary ways of tormenting him.
(Laughs)

MARIANNE Is there no way out?

KATARINA I can't see any.

MARIANNE   Have you talked to Peter?

KATARINA   How sweet you are.

MARIANNE   What does he say?

KATARINA   He says I can do whatever I damn well please. The only thing that interests him slightly is to see just how much we can degrade each other. He calls it our dehumanizing process.

MARIANNE   Do you think he needs a doctor?

KATARINA   He went and had himself analyzed for a while, but he got fed up and said the psychiatrist was an idiot.

MARIANNE   Can't you just walk out on him?

KATARINA   One morning when I woke up the bed was empty. Do you know where he'd gone?

MARIANNE   No.

KATARINA   He was standing out on the ledge, eight floors up, looking down into the street. When I asked him to come in, he said not to worry. I said I wished he would commit suicide. His reply to that was that I wasn't getting out of it all that easily.

MARIANNE   But wasn't there a time when things were good between you?

KATARINA   I'll tell you something that surprises even me. In the middle of it all I feel a hopeless affection for him. I think I understand his misery and disgust and panic and that aching void he feels. And I have an idea that in some strange way he knows things about me that no one else does. He says jokingly that I look like a woman but am a man inside.

(Laughs) In one way he's right. Shall we go back? I'm much better now.

(They rejoin JOHAN *and* PETER, *who have been playing chess in the living room. But* JOHAN *was soon beaten and both tired of it.* JOHAN *serves drinks of various kinds.* MARIANNE *lights a fire)*

PETER *(Rather drunk)* Actually it's all too goddamn touching.

JOHAN What is?

PETER Your marriage. Johan and Marianne. Marianne and Johan. It's so moving it brings a lump to your throat. In fact it makes you want to stick a pin into your beautiful balloon. Skoal to you both!

KATARINA   You've been married for ten years, haven't you?

MARIANNE   We've just had our tenth anniversary.

PETER   And no skeletons in the closet.

JOHAN   *(Laughs)*   Well, you never know.

KATARINA   No, you never know.

MARIANNE   Both Johan and I like to keep things tidy.

PETER   Do you hear that, Katarina? We've been a bit too slov-
enly, you and I. But now we'll get down to it, won't we,
Katarina? Next week I'll call up Marianne and make an
appointment and she can arrange our divorce.

KATARINA   *(Also rather drunk)*   Unfortunately Peter will have
changed his mind before he has sobered up. That's when the
calculating machine starts going clickety-clack. This is what
it says: I'll agree to a divorce if Katarina gives up her claim
on the assets in Switzerland. And my reply is: It's actually
my money. I'm the one who earned it. Then Peter answers
that he's the one who has multiplied it, and I can have the
whole goddamn factory. Thanks, I say, that's nice of you,
what do I want with a factory in Italy that gets to be more
and more of a gamble with every increase in labor costs? So
Peter says, well, you can take the whole damn kit and caboo-
dle in Sweden with apartment and country place and weekend cottage and boats and cars and paintings and stocks and
bonds. And I say, how sweet of you to let me shoulder a
gigantic load of taxable assets. I'm sorry to take up our nice
time together with such trivial matters, but when Peter
starts talking about settling, I know exactly how much he
has had to drink and exactly how much further it will go
before the insults.

PETER   It's just what I'm always saying. Katarina is a businessman, with equal stress on both words. What's more, she's a brilliant artist. What's more, she has an IQ of I don't know what. Pretty, too. She's a paragon, all gift-wrapped. How this monster of perfection has ever allowed me to get between her legs is a mystery.

KATARINA   I think we'll phone for a cab and go home now, Peter. It can't be very pleasant for Johan and Marianne to witness this scene.

PETER *(Carried away)*   Johan and Marianne have red ribbons around their tummies and big bows on their backs, just like the marzipan pigs of our childhood. It's very good for their morale to peep into the bottom-most pit of hell. I wonder whether there's anything more horrible than a husband and wife who hate each other? What do you think? Perhaps child abuse is worse. But then Katarina and I *are* two children, for Chrissake. Right inside Katarina a little girl's sitting and crying because she has fallen and hurt herself and no one has come to comfort her. And I'm sitting in the corner and haven't grown up, and am crying because Katarina can't love me even though I'm nasty to her.

KATARINA   There's one thing to be grateful for. And that is that you can be certain there's nothing worse than this. That's why I think we're ready for divorce.

PETER   Provided you listen to reason. Provided we simultaneously in each other's presence and together with reliable witnesses sign all the papers. So that one of us can't cheat the other. We'll call you this week.

MARIANNE   I'd be glad to help you. And we have an excellent business lawyer at the office. Borglund, you may have heard of him. He can help you with the financial arrangements.

PETER   Well, Katarina, what do you say?

KATARINA   Even if we agree about the money you'll never let me go. I know that.

PETER   Do you imagine you're so indispensable, my dear Katarina? What has suddenly given you that idea? It would be interesting to know. Do tell me.

KATARINA   At any rate, you force me to have sex with you, as you say you can't get an erection with any other woman.

PETER   Your need of a bad conscience is unlimited, and now that it's all over with Jan you're in rather a panic, aren't you, Katarina? You have only old Peter now to bother about you. He has the right kind of patience.

KATARINA   Oh, so you think you're the only one, do you? How touching. You think I have no one else. Let me tell you this, Peter—please excuse me, you two, if I'm rather outspoken, but Peter is asking for it and he needs a little information. I'll tell you this, Peter, you nauseate me so much, I mean physically, that I'd *buy* myself a lay anywhere at all just to wash you out of my sex organs.

PETER   *(Declaiming)*
"Abide with me; fast falls the eventide,
The darkness deepens; Lord with me abide . . ."

KATARINA   You son of a bitch—

PETER   *(Declaiming)*
"When other helpers fail, and comforts flee,
Help of the helpless, O abide with me."
(KATARINA *throws her glass of brandy at* PETER, *who bursts out laughing and dries himself with his handkerchief.* KATARINA *runs sobbing out of the room.* MARIANNE *hurries after her.* JOHAN *starts picking up the splinters of glass from the carpet)* I hope there won't be any stains on the carpet. I don't really know about brandy. If there are any, you can send me the bill. Could I

have some coffee? I'm plastered. Please excuse us, Johan. We don't usually behave like this. But you happen to be our friends. Our only friends. Forgive me. Forgive us. If you will call a cab, I'll take my maenad home and we'll go on with our little scene and finish it there. The finale isn't usually suitable for an audience.

———

Later that evening. The guests have gone.

JOHAN   What are you thinking about?

MARIANNE   Oh, lots of things.

JOHAN   Anything in particular?

MARIANNE   About Katarina and Peter, of course.

JOHAN   So am I.

MARIANNE   Do you think there is any way that two people can live together all their lives?

JOHAN   It's a damned absurd convention that we've inherited from I don't know what. People should have a five-year contract. Or one that is valid from year to year, so that they could give notice.

MARIANNE   Should *we* have one?

JOHAN   No, not us.

MARIANNE   Why not?

JOHAN   You and I are the exception that proves the rule.

We've drawn the winning ticket. In the big idiot lottery.

MARIANNE   So you think we'll live together all our lives?

JOHAN   What a funny question.

MARIANNE   Aren't you ever sorry that you won't sleep with anyone else but me?

JOHAN   Are you?

MARIANNE   Sometimes.

JOHAN *(Astounded)*   I'll be damned.

MARIANNE   But it's a purely theoretical longing.

JOHAN   I wonder if there's something wrong with me, that I never have ideas like that. I'm content.

MARIANNE   So am I. Now I've got it!

JOHAN   What?

MARIANNE   Now I know why Katarina and Peter go through such hell.

JOHAN   Oh?

MARIANNE   They don't speak the same language. They must translate into a third language they both understand in order to get each other's meaning.

JOHAN   I think it's simpler than that.

MARIANNE   Think of us. We talk everything over and we understand each other instantly. We speak the same language. That's why we have such a good relationship.

JOHAN   I think it's the money.

MARIANNE   If they spoke the same language and trusted each other, as we do, the money wouldn't be a problem.

JOHAN   You and your languages.

MARIANNE   I'm always coming across it in my work. Sometimes it's as if husband and wife were making a long-distance call to one another on faulty telephones. Sometimes it's like hearing two tape recorders with preset programs. And sometimes it's the great silence of outer space. I don't know which is most horrible.

JOHAN   All the same, I'm not so sure.

MARIANNE   You always confuse the issue.

JOHAN   Suppose that you and I worked at a factory. Suppose we had the kids at a day nursery. That we worked in shifts, or something like that.

MARIANNE   It would make no difference.

JOHAN   I think it would.

MARIANNE   Those who speak the same language understand each other wherever they are.

JOHAN   It all sounds very romantic to me.

MARIANNE   Do you really think we'd be worse off together if we lived that kind of life? Do you mean that seriously?

JOHAN   Yes, I do. Seriously.

MARIANNE   That things would be worse between us?

JOHAN   Yes, I really mean it. Languages apart.

MARIANNE   Don't you think the danger of loneliness and estrangement is just as great in the life we live?

JOHAN   Definitely not. People doing heavy, dull work are exposed to a much greater strain. It goes without saying, Marianne!

MARIANNE   You're sillier than I thought. And it's you who are romantic.

JOHAN   We'll see.

MARIANNE *(Impatient)* Oh? What will we see?

JOHAN I don't know. Do you?

MARIANNE You're teasing me.

JOHAN Yes, I am. Aren't you hungry?

MARIANNE Yes, terribly.

JOHAN What about some beer and sandwiches?

MARIANNE Sounds marvelous.

———

MARIANNE Come and sit here on the sofa, Johan. There's something I must talk to you about. No, don't look so alarmed. It's nothing very serious.

JOHAN I don't like the sound of this.

MARIANNE Won't you have a brandy?

JOHAN What about you?

MARIANNE Yes, I think I will. You can pour me out one too.

JOHAN Do you mind if I smoke?

MARIANNE No, do. It doesn't matter in the least. I can stand it more now.

JOHAN I think I'll sit down to this. Skoal.

MARIANNE Skoal.

JOHAN Well, what do you want to tell me?

MARIANNE   I'm pregnant.

JOHAN   That's what I said three weeks ago. And you denied it.

MARIANNE   I didn't want to worry you.

JOHAN   I'm not a bit worried.

MARIANNE   What are we going to do about it?

JOHAN   You mean you want an abortion?

MARIANNE   I want us to talk it over. Then we'll do what we've both decided.

JOHAN   I think it's for you to say.

MARIANNE   Why is it up to me?

JOHAN   Well, naturally. You'll have all the discomfort and the onus. Alternatively, the joy and the satisfaction.

MARIANNE   You mean it's all the same to you if we have another child?

JOHAN   I wouldn't put it like that.

MARIANNE   I want to know what you think. Give me a straight answer.

JOHAN   It's not so easy.

MARIANNE   Is it so hard to be honest?

JOHAN   You're being unreasonable now, Marianne.

MARIANNE   What was your first impulse?

JOHAN   It's not in my nature to have first impulses. In that respect I'm an invalid.

MARIANNE   Do you *want* another child?

JOHAN   I have no objections anyway. It might even be rather nice.

MARIANNE   But you can't pretend you're enthusiastic. Can you? Be honest now.

JOHAN   Christ, you keep harping on *my* being honest. Can't you tell me what *you* want instead? It would be much simpler.

MARIANNE   I happened to ask you.

JOHAN   I'm trying to think when we slipped up over the wretched kid. You've been on the pill the whole time. Or haven't you?

MARIANNE   I forgot to take it that time we were away.

JOHAN   Did you now. Why didn't you say so?

MARIANNE   I didn't think it mattered.

JOHAN   Did you do it on purpose?

MARIANNE   I don't know.

JOHAN   That's no answer.

MARIANNE   I suppose I thought, if I get pregnant now, then we're meant to have another child.

JOHAN   Oh my God! My God! My God!

MARIANNE   What's wrong?

JOHAN   And you're supposed to be a modern, efficient professional woman who is always going on about how important family planning is. My God!

MARIANNE   I agree it's rather irrational.

JOHAN   Then you've made up your mind. And in that case there's nothing to be done. Is there?

MARIANNE   I thought you might be pleased.

JOHAN   Oh yes, I'm quite pleased.

MARIANNE   It's the third month.

JOHAN   You haven't been sick at all.

MARIANNE   On the contrary. I've never felt so well.

JOHAN   Our mothers will be overjoyed, at any rate. What do you think our daughters will say?

MARIANNE   Their tolerance is unlimited at the moment. So one act of folly here or there on our part makes no difference. They will forgive us.

JOHAN   Well, well. Skoal, Marianne. And here's welcome to him or her. You know, I'm quite beginning to look forward to it. Besides, you're so pretty when you're big-bellied. *(A long silence ensues. Then* MARIANNE *begins to weep.* JOHAN *looks at her astonished)*   What's wrong now?

MARIANNE   Nothing.

JOHAN   There must be something.

MARIANNE   No, nothing, really.

JOHAN   Just what do you want yourself?

MARIANNE   I don't know.

JOHAN   What it really amounts to is that neither you nor I
want any more children.

MARIANNE   Do you think so?

JOHAN   I think we're both appalled at the thought of a squall-
ing brat and feedings and diapers and nursing and getting
up at night and the whole damn circus. We like to think
that's all behind us.

MARIANNE   I have such a bad conscience.

JOHAN   Why?

MARIANNE   I have a bad conscience because first I go and long
for a child and toy with the idea and look forward to it, and
then, when it's a fact, I regret it no end. It doesn't make
sense.

JOHAN   Why must you be so moral about it all?

MARIANNE   It's my fourth child, Johan. One died, and I take
the life of another.

JOHAN   Good God, you can't reason like that.

MARIANNE   I do, anyway.

JOHAN   It's a question of being practical.

MARIANNE   No, it isn't.

JOHAN   What, then?

MARIANNE   It's a question of love.

JOHAN   Aren't you too worked up now?

MARIANNE   No.

JOHAN   Then can't you explain what you mean?

MARIANNE   No, I can't, because it's a feeling. It's as if I no longer felt I was real. You're not real either. Nor are the children. Then along comes this baby. *That*'s real.

JOHAN   You might say just the opposite.

MARIANNE   We're too comfortable, that's the trouble, and then we're left with our wretched cowardice and unreality and shame. And we have no affection either. And no love. And no joy. We could easily welcome this baby. And I think I was right in looking forward to it when I went around daydreaming about it. I had the right feeling. I'd be *ready* now to have a baby.

JOHAN   I don't know what you're talking about.

MARIANNE   No.

JOHAN   You speak as if you'd already had an abortion.

MARIANNE   In one way I have.

JOHAN   One can't blame oneself for thoughts.

MARIANNE   (*Shouting*)   This is serious, Johan. *The whole of our future's at stake.* Suppose we now do something irrevocable. Suppose it's crucial and we don't know it is.

JOHAN   What are these ridiculous, ghostly, intangible demands you're making? They're pure superstition.

MARIANNE   You don't understand.

JOHAN   No, I'm damned if I do understand a single word of what you've been saying.

MARIANNE   We're only trying to get out of it.

JOHAN   We're trying to avoid dramatic decisions and anything rash, if that's what you mean. And I think that's sensible. (*Gives* MARIANNE *a glum look*)

MARIANNE   You don't look so happy either.

JOHAN   This conversation makes me feel sick.

MARIANNE   Johan!

JOHAN   Yes?

MARIANNE   Couldn't we have this baby and look forward to it? Couldn't we spoil it a little and be fond of it just because we were careless about it?

JOHAN   I've already said it would be nice, so there's no need to harp on it. You're the one who has made it all so complicated. Not I.

MARIANNE   Let's make up our minds then.

JOHAN   About what?

MARIANNE   Let's decide to have another baby.

JOHAN   Well, that's that.

MARIANNE   I feel quite relieved.

JOHAN *(Kindly)*   There's nothing so strange about both wanting to and not wanting to.

MARIANNE   No, I suppose not.

JOHAN   If anything, it's the rule.

MARIANNE   Actually, it had nothing to do with the baby.

JOHAN   No, I suppose not.

MARIANNE   It had to do with you and me.

JOHAN   You're not still crying?

MARIANNE   I don't know what's the matter with me.

JOHAN   I think you need a brandy.

MARIANNE   Yes, I think I do.

———

Some time later. MARIANNE *is lying in a bed.* JOHAN *comes in and sits down. He takes her hand.*

JOHAN   How do you feel?

MARIANNE   Oh, all right.

JOHAN   Was it difficult?

MARIANNE   Not particularly.

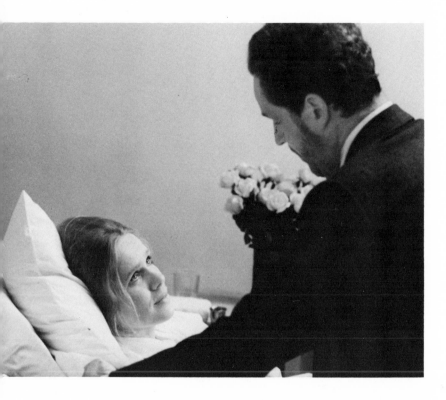

JOHAN The doctor said you could come home tomorrow, or the day after at the latest.

MARIANNE I'm going to sleep and sleep.

JOHAN I thought you and I would go down to the country for a week when you're fit. I think I can take some time off after the tenth. I phoned your mother and asked if she'd mind looking after the girls and she was delighted. So that's no obstacle.

MARIANNE   It *would* be rather nice.

JOHAN   I had dinner with Göran and Sven yesterday. They think that Sture will be made ambassador to Pretoria of all places. I wonder what Aina will say to *that* appointment. What a blow to her pride! And imagine not being able to take tea with Princess Sibylla on Fridays. She'll never survive that.

MARIANNE   When is it to be decided?

JOHAN   Any day now.

MARIANNE   By the way, have you phoned the Egermans at Högsätra and told them we can't come to dinner?

JOHAN   No, I forgot. I'll do it right away.

MARIANNE   Have you talked to our parents?

JOHAN   I said that you had had a minor operation and that it was all rather sudden because the doctor was going abroad.

MARIANNE   What did Mother say?

JOHAN   She sniffled with sympathy and might be here any moment.

MARIANNE   That's what I'm afraid of.

JOHAN   If you like I'll call her up and ask her to come some other time. I can say you're asleep.

MARIANNE   No, that will only make it worse.

JOHAN   Is it hurting?

MARIANNE   I'm just a little sore.

JOHAN   I thought we'd talk about the country house. Do you feel up to it? Or would you rather . . .

MARIANNE   Yes, of course I do.

JOHAN   What about building on a nice rustic veranda to the house? And painting it blue?

MARIANNE   Shouldn't we repaint the house too?

JOHAN   Yes, I did think of it. And sooner or later we must retile the roof. It won't last much longer.

MARIANNE   Can we afford it?

JOHAN   It won't cost an awful lot.

MARIANNE   You'd better speak to Gustav about it.

JOHAN   Yes, I'll have a word with Gustav.
   (Silence)

MARIANNE   Johan.

JOHAN   Yes, darling?

MARIANNE   Hold my hand, will you?

JOHAN   Does that feel better?

MARIANNE   Yes.

JOHAN   Good.

MARIANNE   *(Whispering)*   Johan.

JOHAN   Yes?

MARIANNE   I feel such awful remorse. (JOHAN *makes no reply, holds her hand*) I can't tell you how awful.

JOHAN   You'll feel better tomorrow.

MARIANNE   *What have I done?*

JOHAN   There's no point in thinking like that.

MARIANNE   No.

JOHAN   In a few weeks you'll have forgotten all about it.

MARIANNE   Do you think so?

JOHAN   I'm quite sure you will.

MARIANNE   Johan.

JOHAN   Yes?

MARIANNE   I don't know how I shall get over it.

JOHAN   Won't you try and get some sleep?

MARIANNE   Yes.

JOHAN   I must go now anyway. Look after yourself.

MARIANNE   Bye-bye. Give my love to the girls.

JOHAN   Sleep well. If your mother comes, I'll ask the nurse to say you're asleep.

MARIANNE   Maybe it's just as well. You can try to call her. So she doesn't come all the way for nothing.

JOHAN   Yes, I will.

MARIANNE You're so kind.

JOHAN I'm glad you think so.

MARIANNE We'll have a nice time in the country.

JOHAN Eating and sleeping and watching TV. And not thinking.

MARIANNE We'll sit and hold hands.

JOHAN Sleep well.

MARIANNE Don't forget to call up the Egermans.

JOHAN No, I won't forget.
(MARIANNE *is left alone. She closes her eyes but can't get to sleep. She lies staring at the ceiling. Her eyes fill with tears. She sighs over and over again*)

SECOND SCENE

The Art
of Sweeping
Under the Rug

CHARACTERS

JOHAN
MARIANNE
KARIN AND EVA, their daughters
MRS. JACOBI
SECRETARY
EVA

MARIANNE   Good morning.

JOHAN   Good morning.

MARIANNE   Did you sleep well?

JOHAN   Like a log. And you?

MARIANNE   Oh, so-so. Stupidly I woke up at five o'clock and couldn't get back to sleep.

JOHAN   Why not?

MARIANNE   I lay there getting all worked up.

JOHAN   Should I have a bad conscience?

MARIANNE   For once you're not to blame, my darling. I lay fuming about that wretched Sunday dinner with my parents.

JOHAN   But we always have Sunday dinner with our parents. Either yours or mine.

MARIANNE   It's utterly absurd.

JOHAN   We do it for their sake.

MARIANNE   I'm going to call anyway and say we can't come.

JOHAN   Can't come! Whatever will your mother say?

MARIANNE   She can say what she darn well pleases. You and I are going to have a nice Sunday to ourselves together with the children.

JOHAN   Well, if you can accomplish *that!*

MARIANNE   I'm beginning to lose my temper.

JOHAN   Is it the curse?

MARIANNE   You always think it's that.

JOHAN   Well, isn't it?

MARIANNE   Even if my period *is* due on Monday, that's not necessarily why I feel like blowing my top.

JOHAN   But Marianne dear, what is it?

MARIANNE   Just think about it. Our life's mapped out into little squares—every day, every hour, every minute. And on every square it's written down what we're supposed to do. The squares are filled one by one and in good time. If there's suddenly an empty square we're dismayed and scrawl something onto it at once.

JOHAN   But we have our vacation.

MARIANNE   *(With a laugh)*   Johan! You haven't a clue to what I mean. On our vacation we have more of a schedule than ever. It's all Mummy's fault, actually. And your mother's not much better.

JOHAN *(Laughing)*   What have the dear old ladies done wrong?

MARIANNE   You don't understand anyway, so there's no point talking about it.

JOHAN   Aren't you going to wake up the girls?

MARIANNE   No, they're having a late morning. Karin has the day off from school and Eva had rather a sore throat last night, so I thought I'd let her stay home. *(Angry)* So that she can come with us to dinner on Sunday. Otherwise there'll be a hell of a fuss with comments and questions. You must admit.

JOHAN   You were going to phone and say we can't come.

MARIANNE   I'd rather you did.

JOHAN   Oh no, thank you! I'm not getting tangled up in making excuses to your mother. You can do that yourself.

MARIANNE   Then I'm going to call up your sister and tell her I don't want to go with her to the fashion show on Friday. Then I'm going to send our regrets to the Bergmans about dinner on Friday. They'll be madly hurt but I don't give a damn. Then you can refuse the invitation to the Peruvian ambassador's cocktail party. And I have no intention of going to your mother's French course, nor am I going to the theater this evening. And you can take next week off and we'll go away somewhere together. *(With tears in her eyes)* Oh God, how stupid. This isn't the way to solve problems.

JOHAN *(Kindly)*   What is it you want then?

MARIANNE *(Shaking her head)*   I can't express it. We work hard, both of us. It isn't that. We're always meeting people. There's nothing wrong with that either. We spend time with our children as often as we can. That too is just as it should be. We hardly ever quarrel, and if we do we're sensible and listen to each other and make a valid compromise. Things couldn't be better.

JOHAN It sounds ideal.

MARIANNE It's troubling all the same.

JOHAN *(Smiling)* And our mothers are to blame.

MARIANNE Yes, I think so, though I can't prove it.

JOHAN   Then we can only express a pious wish that the dear ladies die as soon as possible.

MARIANNE *(Earnestly)*   Someone should have killed them long ago!

JOHAN   For that matter, doesn't the Bible say . . .

MARIANNE *(Absent-mindedly)*   Hmm? What does the Bible say?

JOHAN   "Therefore shall a man leave his father and his mother, and shall cleave unto his wife, and they shall be one flesh." Call up your mother now. She's a horribly early riser.

MARIANNE   Didn't we agree that *you* were going to make our excuses?

JOHAN   Oh no, my darling. Go on, call her. I'll hold your hand and be your moral support.

MARIANNE   All right, I will. Feel how my heart's pounding. But sooner or later we must take the first step.

JOHAN   The first faint cries of the great revolution. No answer? What a relief!

MARIANNE   Hello. Good morning, Miss Alm. Is Mother there? Oh, good. May I have a word with her? By the way, Miss Alm, how is your knee? Oh, not any better. Is it worse? Oh, I *am* sorry. What does the doctor say? Not much sympathy, eh? No, that's how it is these days. *(With a change of tone)* Good morning, Mummy. How are you? That's good to hear. Has Daddy gone yet? Oh yes, of course, he was going to the country. Can you let him go off on his own like that? Oh, Erik's with him. That's good. Er, Mummy, I have something to tell you. I'm awfully sorry, but . . . *(Long pause, while her mother speaks)* Yes, how did you guess? What are our reasons? I just want to be alone with Johan and the children

for a whole Sunday. No, we're not going anywhere. No, we just don't want to come to dinner. *(Her mother talks)* I don't think for a moment that Daddy was looking forward to Sunday dinner. *(Her mother talks)* Yes, but Mummy, it should be a pleasure, not a duty. *(Her mother talks)* Yes, I see. I see. I didn't know that. You didn't tell me. *(Her mother talks)* Bored stiff, to be quite honest. No, no, forget all about it, Mummy. No, no, please! *(Her mother talks)* We'll come as arranged. Yes, we'll manage. Yes, that's all right. Johan sends his love. Bye for now, Mummy dear.
(She puts down the phone)

JOHAN   The revolution was smothered at birth.

MARIANNE   Aunt Elsa was coming to dinner. She hasn't been up to town for over six months. And she was *particularly* looking forward to seeing us. And she was bringing a present for you. *(Angry)* Damnation!

JOHAN   And your mother had asked Mrs. Danielson to come and cook the dinner. And your father was *so* looking forward to seeing us.

MARIANNE   Hell and damnation!

JOHAN   I admire your pluck all the same. *(Kisses her)* We'll say no some other time. Don't upset yourself.

MARIANNE   Will you be home for dinner?

JOHAN   No, we'd better meet at the theater. Let's say twenty past seven at the righthand box office. I'll be there in plenty of time to pick up the tickets.

MARIANNE   It's a funny thing, you know.

JOHAN   What's funny?

MARIANNE   Do you like coming home?

JOHAN *(Kindly)*   Is everything so awfully complicated today?

MARIANNE   I'd like us to hide in bed and just hold each other tight and not get up for a whole week. And we'd both have a good cry.

JOHAN   We haven't chosen that sort of life.

MARIANNE   If only I were sure that it's we who have chosen, and not our mothers.

JOHAN   You're suffering from mother persecution mania.

MARIANNE   Did you *want* your life to be like this?

JOHAN   I think that life has the value you give it, neither more nor less. I refuse to live under the eye of eternity.

MARIANNE   Imagine if you and I started being unfaithful to each other.

JOHAN *(Embarrassed)*   Why, Marianne!

MARIANNE   I don't mean temporarily. But all the time. I mean if we seriously fell in love with someone else. What would you say?

JOHAN   I'd kill you of course.

MARIANNE *(With a sigh)*   Sometimes I wish . . .

JOHAN   What?

MARIANNE   Nothing. *(Kiss)* So long, darling!

JOHAN   So long!

MARIANNE   Wait a second, Johan. I'll come with you.

JOHAN   Wouldn't it be better if you took your own car?

MARIANNE   No, I'm staying in town too. Then we'll drive home together after the theater this evening. It's much better.

JOHAN   What about the girls?

MARIANNE   Mrs. Andersson's coming to clean today. I'll phone home and ask her to give them something to eat. She makes wonderful pancakes. Wait, I'll just go in and wake up the children.

JOHAN   But I'm in a hurry.

MARIANNE   It won't take a minute.
(MARIANNE *hurries into the girls' room and is heard rousing two sleepy princesses on their peas.* JOHAN *picks up the phone but changes his mind and puts it down again. At the same moment* MARIANNE *is back. She has grabbed a briefcase and* JOHAN *helps her on with her coat. Then off they go. It is pouring rain)*

JOHAN   I'll snatch a bite on the way to the theater.

MARIANNE   Don't forget the dentist today at three o'clock. Last time—

JOHAN   I forgot. I know, you've told me four times now. By the way, I have to leave the car to be serviced. One of the rear lights is broken.

MARIANNE   I do enjoy driving with you. We should do it more often. Did it put you out my asking to come with you?

JOHAN   I don't like improvisations, you know that.

MARIANNE   I'm just the opposite. Sometimes I'd like to take the day just as it comes. Eat when I'm hungry, sleep when I'm sleepy, make love when I feel desire. Perhaps even do some work, when the mood strikes me. Sometimes I have an irresistible urge just to drift, perhaps sink.

JOHAN   Who doesn't?

MARIANNE   *You.* You don't have that urge.

JOHAN *(Sharply all of a sudden)*   How do you know?

MARIANNE *(With a smile)*   No, my sweet, I think I know you pretty well by now. You're far too methodical to get ideas like that. You love everything neat and tidy.

JOHAN   So do you.

MARIANNE   I don't know. Do I?

JOHAN   You're as pedantic as they come.

MARIANNE   You don't say so.

JOHAN   You hate mental and physical untidiness.

MARIANNE   Oh, do I. Well, well.

JOHAN   So there.

MARIANNE   I'm not as certain as you are.

JOHAN   Of what?

MARIANNE   Who I really am.

JOHAN   Before I forget, for goodness' sake pay your parking tickets. You have a whole sheaf of them in the car now. It's quite unnecessary.

MARIANNE   Yes, sir. Heavens, what a downpour. I should have brought an umbrella. And I don't have the right shoes either.

JOHAN   Well, here we are.
(*The lawyers' office is on a small, quiet street.* MARIANNE *gives her husband a peck on the cheek and gets out of the car.* JOHAN *waves to her and drives off. It's raining heavily and* MARIANNE *hurries into the doorway and up the stairs of the dignified old house with its gleaming banisters, stained-glass staircase windows, and heavy marble walls. She nods to the secretary and the day's first client, who is already sitting waiting. Once inside her room she changes her shoes, hangs up her jacket, and puts on a sweater. She asks the client to come in*)

MARIANNE   How do you do, Mrs. Jacobi. Please sit down. At this first meeting we usually try just to pose the actual problem. Then we'll see how we can solve it.

MRS. JACOBI   I want a divorce.

MARIANNE   How long have you been married?

MRS. JACOBI   I've been married for twenty years.

MARIANNE   Have you worked outside your home?

MRS. JACOBI   No, I've been a housewife, as it's called.

MARIANNE   How many children do you have?

MRS. JACOBI   We have three children. They're grown up now. The youngest is doing his national service. The oldest, a girl, is married and the younger girl is in college and doesn't live at home.

MARIANNE   Then you're alone now?

MRS. JACOBI   I have my husband, of course.

MARIANNE *(Smiling)*   Of course. Is he at home all the time?

MRS. JACOBI   No, he's a schoolteacher.

MARIANNE   Why do you want a divorce?

MRS. JACOBI   It's a loveless marriage.

MARIANNE   Is *that* your reason?

MRS. JACOBI   Yes.

MARIANNE *(Cautiously)*   But you've been married for such a long time. Has it always been like that, or . . .

MRS. JACOBI   Yes, it has always been like that.

MARIANNE   And now that the children have left home you want to break away. Is that right?

MRS. JACOBI   My husband is very dependable. I have no fault to find with him. He is kind and conscientious. He has been an excellent father. We have never quarreled. We have a nice apartment and a pleasant old house in the country that was left to us by his mother. We're both interested in music and are members of a chamber music society—we play together ourselves.

MARIANNE   It all sounds ideal.

MRS. JACOBI   Yes, doesn't it. But there is no love in the marriage. There never has been.

MARIANNE   Forgive my asking: Have you by any chance met another man?

MRS. JACOBI   No, I haven't.

MARIANNE   And your husband?

MRS. JACOBI   As far as I know he has never been unfaithful.

MARIANNE   Won't it be rather lonely?

MRS. JACOBI   Yes, very likely. But I prefer that loneliness to living in a marriage without love.

MARIANNE   Please forgive another question. What form does this lovelessness take?

MRS. JACOBI   It doesn't take any form.

MARIANNE   Then I don't understand.

MRS. JACOBI   No, it's hard to explain.

MARIANNE   Have you told your husband that you want a divorce?

MRS. JACOBI   Naturally. Fifteen years ago I told him that I didn't want to live with him any longer, as there was no love in our marriage. He was very understanding. He merely asked me to wait for the divorce until the children were grown up. Now all three have grown up and left home. So now I can get my divorce.

MARIANNE   And what does your husband say?

MRS. JACOBI   He wants me to think it over carefully. He has asked me hundreds of times what is wrong with our marriage, that I want to leave him. I've told him it's impossible to continue a relationship in which there is no love. Then he asks me what this love is supposed to consist of. And I've answered him a hundred times that I don't know, for it's impossible to describe something that doesn't exist.

MARIANNE   Have you been on good terms with your children?
I mean emotionally.

MRS. JACOBI   I have never loved my children. I know that for
sure. But I've been quite a good mother all the same. I've
done all I could, although I've never actually felt anything
for them. *(Smiles)* I know just what you're thinking.

MARIANNE *(Caught)*   Oh, really? Are you a mind reader?

MRS. JACOBI   You're thinking: That Mrs. Jacobi is a spoiled
woman if ever I saw one. She has everything one could wish
for in this world but never stops feeling sorry for herself and
fussing about something vague and remote which she calls
love. There are other things, after all: comradeship, loyalty,
affection, friendship, wellbeing, security.

MARIANNE   I *was* perhaps thinking something of the kind.

MRS. JACOBI   Let me tell you something. I go around with a
mental picture of myself. And it doesn't tally on a single
point with reality.

MARIANNE   May I ask a personal question, Mrs. Jacobi? Isn't
it true of love that . . .

MRS. JACOBI   What were you going to say?

MARIANNE   I don't know.

MRS. JACOBI   I tell myself that I have the capacity for love, but
it's all bottled up inside me. The trouble is that the life I have
lived up to now has just stifled my potentialities more and
more. At last I must do something about it. So my first step
must be to get a divorce. I think my husband and I are
hindering each other in a—fatal way.

MARIANNE   It sounds frightening.

MRS. JACOBI   It *is* frightening. Something most peculiar is happening: my senses—I mean feeling, sight, hearing—are starting to fail me. For instance, I can say that this table is a table, I can see it, I can touch it. But the sensation is thin and dry, if you can understand.

MARIANNE   *(Suddenly)*   I think I do.

MRS. JACOBI   It's the same with everything else. Music, scents, people's faces and voices. Everything's getting meaner and grayer, with no dignity.

MARIANNE   Do you think now that you will meet some other man?

MRS. JACOBI   *(With a smile)*   No, I don't. I have no illusions.

MARIANNE   Can you make your husband understand this breaking away?

MRS. JACOBI   He only gets bitter and bad-tempered and says I'm romantic and silly and suffering from change of life.

MARIANNE   The best thing would be if you could get your husband to agree willingly to a divorce.

MRS. JACOBI   He says he's refusing for my sake. I'll regret it, he says.

MARIANNE   But you've made up your mind?

MRS. JACOBI   I have no choice. Do you understand what I mean?

MARIANNE   *(Evasively)*   I think so. *(Suddenly Marianne remembers something and asks Mrs. Jacobi to excuse her for a moment. She goes*

*into the outer office and makes a call on the secretary's phone. Johan
answers)* Hello. Sorry to disturb you.

JOHAN   It doesn't matter.

MARIANNE   I wondered if we could have lunch together.

JOHAN   Yes, if you like. I'm going to just grab a sandwich at
twelve thirty.

MARIANNE   Where is it you usually go? The grill bar, isn't it?
I'll see you there just after twelve thirty. Bye!

━━━━━

JOHAN *in the laboratory. He is standing on a small metal stepladder,
photographing bit values on square white cardboard targets. The telephone rings. He mutters an oath, gets down reluctantly, and answers.*

JOHAN   Hello. Yes, speaking. Why, hello, Mother, I didn't
hear it was you at first, the phone's crackling. Oh, I'm fine.
How are you? You're worried? What do you mean by that?
Has Marianne's mother called? Now what's all this. Is she
worried too? Good heavens! No, no, no, I assure you. Everything's just fine with Marianne and me. We're strong and
healthy and cheerful and optimistic and madly happy together. Nothing whatever has happened. I swear. Mother
dear, don't *worry*. Your intuition? Well, it has led you astray
this time, I can assure you. Everything is just fine between
Marianne and me. I think you ought to call up Marianne's
mother and tell her she ought to know better than to gossip
with you on the phone. Look, Mother, I'm in rather a hurry
just now. Yes, yes, I'll see you soon. We'll drop by on Friday
as agreed. Give my love to Father. *(Hangs up)* Phew! Hell
and damnation! *(He climbs up the ladder and resumes work. There
is a knock at the door)* Come in.

EVA   Hello.

JOHAN   Hello.

EVA   Am I disturbing you?

JOHAN   Yes, but I'm glad of it.

EVA   I just wanted to see what you're up to. I've heard the most extraordinary rumors about your doings. *(Looks about her)* Whatever is all this? It does look mysterious.

JOHAN   Shouldn't you be in Lund?

EVA   Yes, by rights. But the students are demonstrating for some deserving cause or other, so the lectures were canceled.

JOHAN   How nice.

EVA   Yes, so here I am. Just what are you up to? Do tell me.

JOHAN   Look for yourself.

EVA   What do I do?

JOHAN   Take this pen in your right hand. When I put the light out you'll see a brightly shining fixed dot on the wall in front of you. Try to touch it with the point of the pen. If you miss it you must draw a line until you reach it. This TV camera will register your efforts on a monitor. Off you go. *(The experiment is carried out. Toward the end* EVA *is quite annoyed at not hitting the dot)*

EVA   I've had enough of this. Please put the light on.

JOHAN   Aren't you cross!

EVA   Well, it was a bit nerve-racking.

JOHAN   Yes, it does get on your nerves. Funny, isn't it? Look at this—you've wandered all over the place, getting more and more irritated.

EVA   Hmm. And what do we learn from all this?

JOHAN   That remains to be seen. This is only the beginning.

EVA   Oh. I'd like a cigarette.

JOHAN   Sit down.

EVA   I've stopped smoking for six days now. It's awful.

JOHAN   Having abstinence trouble, eh?

EVA   Stefan's away, my friends shun me. I suspect I'll start again but I'll try to stick it out a bit longer.

JOHAN   Go on, have one now. Broméus forgot these when he was in here spying yesterday. There now.

EVA   *(Sighs, takes a cigarette, lights it, inhales luxuriously)*   Oh, that's heaven. God, what bliss! Now I feel better.

JOHAN   Now you'll have a bad conscience and that's nice too. One must seize every chance of enjoyment these days. *(With a smile)* Well?

EVA   Actually, that's why I came.

JOHAN   That's good of you.

EVA   I sat down yesterday afternoon and read your poems very carefully twice.

JOHAN   And?

EVA   I couldn't make head or tail of them.

JOHAN   Was that so strange?

EVA   On the contrary.

JOHAN   It wasn't strange?
(Smiles ruefully)

EVA   I don't know, maybe I'm wrong. Has Marianne read the poems?

JOHAN   No, you're the only one I've shown them to. Marianne's not interested in poetry.

EVA   But she ought to be interested in you.

JOHAN   *(Crossly)*   Oh, she is, but not quite in that way.

EVA   *(Looks at him with a smile)*   Oh, I see. No.

JOHAN   Well, what's so odd about it? You and I have known each other since we were students. We're not lovers. From you I can get an objective opinion before going to a publisher and trying to get the poems printed.

EVA   I wouldn't if I were you.

JOHAN   Wouldn't what?

EVA   Go to a publisher.

JOHAN   Are they as bad as that?

EVA   It's not that they're bad, Johan. If only they *were*, I was going to say.

JOHAN   You mean they're mediocre? (EVA *sighs*) You mean that they're insipid and neat and puerile. You mean that it's just a private gripe. A little mental masturbation.

EVA   I'll tell you something.

JOHAN   Well?

EVA   There were several of us in our set who thought you were going to make a name for yourself. We thought you were phenomenal. You left us all behind and we admired you, even envied you.

JOHAN   What does that have to do with the poems?

EVA   I don't know. It was just a thought.

JOHAN   I have no cause for complaint.

EVA   Well, that's just fine then.

JOHAN   Are you sure you didn't read the poems under the influence of your nicotine craving? You're pretty nervy just now.

EVA   It's quite possible.

JOHAN   Don't you think that the whole of this unpleasant situation is caused by your not having smoked for six days?

EVA   Yes, I suppose so.
      (Gives a friendly smile)

JOHAN   I'm going to let others read my poems before I scrap them.

EVA   Why, Johan my dear, of course!

JOHAN   I'm going to send them to several different publishers, to make quite sure of their mediocrity.

EVA   You've really taken offence, haven't you?

JOHAN   You bet I have!

EVA   I'm sorry.

JOHAN   Anyway, there's *one* person who likes my poems.

EVA   Oh, who's that?

JOHAN   That made you curious, eh?

EVA   Well then, Johan. One for, one against. Don't take any notice of what I said. Let's say it's just nicotine craving. Bye-bye, my dear. I'll leave the manuscript with the doorman. My regards to Marianne. *(Turns)* Remember, I'll stick by you through thick and thin. Bye!

JOHAN   Bye-bye.
        (EVA *goes out, leaving* JOHAN *alone in his laboratory. He reaches for the telephone but checks himself. Resumes his photographing)*

━━━━━

The grill bar is poky and crowded. JOHAN *and* MARIANNE *have found an apology for a table by a window.*

MARIANNE   It's ages since we had lunch together. How nice.

JOHAN   And what brings you?

MARIANNE   I think you and I ought to go away together next summer. We've arranged to take our vacation at the same time, so it would be a good idea to go abroad. I popped into one or two travel agents and got all these brochures—look. As long as you book early you can join a cheap package tour. Then once you get there you can do just as you like. It's just that the actual trip is much cheaper.

JOHAN   You mean, we wouldn't be down in the country at all?

MARIANNE   We can be there all the spring and fall.

JOHAN   Where did you think of going?

MARIANNE   Anywhere. We've never been to Florence, for instance. Or what about the Black Sea? That's an idea. Or Africa? There are some fantastically cheap trips to Morocco. Or Japan. Suppose we went to Japan!

JOHAN   Why this sudden urge to travel?

MARIANNE   *(Pause)*   Don't *you* think it would be fun? Just to go off like that?

JOHAN   I don't know.

MARIANNE   Then let's forget it.
(*Gathers up the brochures*)

JOHAN   Are you disappointed?

MARIANNE   When you're in a bad mood you always come out with a very funny accusation: You say I couldn't care less about our marriage. Isn't that what you say? Well, now I *am* caring about it.

JOHAN   How thoughtful of you.

MARIANNE   Why the sarcasm?

JOHAN   It's not sarcasm at all. I do think it's thoughtful. It's just that I don't think I want to trail around foreign parts in the blazing heat. When I could be sitting in a boat fishing.

MARIANNE   It'll all be the same as usual then.

JOHAN   Why not send the children to your sister? That would be a big relief.

MARIANNE   Not if we stay at home.

JOHAN   Why not?

MARIANNE   It would look awfully funny.

JOHAN   So what?

MARIANNE   It won't do. And what do you think Mother would say? She'd grumble and fuss and we'd never hear the end of it. Besides, the children would also think it was funny. Of course, we could ask Valborg to look after them for a week, or ten days at the most, but certainly no more.

JOHAN   Must we be so dependent on what everyone thinks?

MARIANNE   I don't understand what you're getting at.

JOHAN   Marianne . . .

MARIANNE   *(Serious suddenly)*   Yes, Johan.

JOHAN   Do you think life is dull?

MARIANNE   No. What a question! Do you?

JOHAN   I don't know. I've never thought in those terms.

MARIANNE   I still think life's exciting.

JOHAN   *(Looking at her)*   You *are* pretty, you know.

MARIANNE With my hair in a mess, and this awful old jumper, and no make-up . . .

JOHAN Marianne!

MARIANNE Is there something you want to tell me?

JOHAN Can the scheme of things be so treacherous that life suddenly goes wrong? Without your knowing how it happens. Almost imperceptibly.

MARIANNE *(Softly)* Do you mean us?

JOHAN Is it a matter of choosing, and making the wrong choice? Or of jogging along in the same old rut without thinking. Until you lie there on the garbage dump.

MARIANNE *(Searchingly)* Has something happened, Johan?

JOHAN Nothing. Absolutely nothing. I swear.

MARIANNE We're pretty honest with each other, you and I. Aren't we?

JOHAN I think so.

MARIANNE It's awful to go around bottling things up. One must speak out, however painful it is. Don't you think?

JOHAN *(Irritably)* Hell, yes. What time is it?

MARIANNE One fifteen.

JOHAN My watch is always stopping. What were you saying? Oh yes, honesty. I suppose you mean over sex, to put it bluntly.

MARIANNE Sometimes I think we . . .

JOHAN   People can't always live cheek by jowl. It would be too tiring.

MARIANNE   Yes, *that* is the big question.

JOHAN   Anyway, I must go now.

MARIANNE   I'll take a little walk. I have to buy some new slacks for Karin, too.

JOHAN   Good Lord, you bought a pair last week.

MARIANNE   Those were for Eva.

JOHAN   Can't their clothes be handed down? It certainly had to be done in my childhood.

MARIANNE   Well, it's not done nowadays, you see, my poor darling. Bye-bye, see you at the theater.

JOHAN   Yes.

MARIANNE   *(Suddenly)*   I'm so fond of you, do you know that? Do you know that I'm dead scared of losing you? I ought to say nice things to you much more often, I know they mean a lot to you. I'm not very good at it, I'm afraid. I'll try to improve. You're so kind. And I'm very, very fond of you.

JOHAN   I'll try to remember that.

MARIANNE   So long, and drive carefully.

———

MARIANNE *and* JOHAN *are on their way home in the car after having been to a performance of Ibsen's* A Doll's House.

JOHAN   Now for a sandwich and some beer. Having to skip

dinner like that and bolt a hot dog before struggling through a whole evening of Ibsen is enough to kill anyone.

MARIANNE   I thought Nora was good.

JOHAN   Yes, but the play damn well creaks. Even Strindberg thought so.

MARIANNE   He was just jealous.

JOHAN   A few things have happened during the last hundred years, after all. Though not in the way Ibsen hoped.

MARIANNE   Have they?

JOHAN   *(Laughs and yawns)*   Feminism is a worn-out subject, Marianne. Women nowadays can do whatever they like. The trouble is they can't be bothered.

MARIANNE   *(Smiles)*   Oh, that's interesting!

JOHAN   Women pose as martyrs. It's much more convenient. And above all it involves no responsibility when things get hot. I always thought there was something absurd and pathetic about suffragettes, and now Women's Lib. Especially when they try to put some life into their sisters. A parochial, ineffectual, moronic mob who brainwash themselves from birth. It's too damn heartbreaking for words.

MARIANNE   We're only starting. Just you wait and see.

JOHAN   I'll never see anything. There are a couple of middle-aged women at my office who have been sharing the same room for donkey's years. They still address each other as Miss Schoultz and Mrs. Palmgren, and they seize every opportunity of sabotaging each other or running one another down.

MARIANNE   That was a telling argument.

JOHAN   Have you ever heard of a female symphony orchestra? Imagine a hundred and ten women with menstrual trouble trying to play Rossini's overture to *The Thieving Magpie.*

MARIANNE   Lucky no one can hear you.

JOHAN   Women are crazy. Imagine a regular goddamn carcass of a man, an alcoholic, rotten to the core and ready to end it all. I bet you anything that around the remains of this swine a lot of fantastic women will hover like big white birds. The carcass stinks, he ill-treats them—it makes no difference. It's one glorious combination of greedily sparkling eyes, rosy cheeks, and a general air of martyrdom. Some idiot of a man who was champion of women's rights —I think it was a progressive bishop, at that—made out that women have been tyrannized for so long that they have at last accepted their degradation.

MARIANNE   *(With a smile)*   Yes, that was very stupid.

JOHAN   Women pinched the best part at the outset. You bet your sweet life they're not giving it up now that they've learned to play it to perfection. Besides, they've achieved what they've always been after: man's collective bad conscience, which gives them unbelievable advantages without their having to lift a finger. What do women want in parliament or in the government? It would only force them to share a responsibility. They would lose their comfortable role of opposition. They would have to get rid of their pet vices: bringing up children and letting themselves be supported and oppressed. I heard one woman say, "But don't we women have a very special talent for affection?" I was too polite to laugh. But those are the kind of propaganda slogans you women use when you want to wriggle out of a tricky situation. What I'd like to ask is this: Don't women have a very special talent for cruelty, brutality, vulgarity, and ruthlessness? *(Laughs)* I don't mean a word of what I say, and anyway I couldn't care less about it.

━━━

Beer and sandwiches are on the kitchen table. MARIANNE *has taken off her best black dress and put on a white dressing gown made of Turkish toweling.* JOHAN *is sitting in his shirtsleeves.*

MARIANNE   When I got back to the office this afternoon, Elsa —you know, our secretary—was crying on a sofa. Her nose was bleeding and she had a nasty bruise over one eye. She had been attacked in the street by three teen-age louts. In broad daylight. People had stood around watching and never lifted a finger to help. Then a couple of bored-looking police came along and asked questions and told Elsa off for going around with her salary in her pocketbook. They more or less implied that it was her own fault.

JOHAN   Sometimes you feel that the whole community is going to the dogs.

MARIANNE   When we were younger we were so hopeful.

JOHAN   Do you remember when our parents practically turned us out because we joined the May Day procession?

MARIANNE   And we used to go in for amateur dramatics.

JOHAN   You were more religious than I was.

MARIANNE   And you accused me of neglecting my home.

JOHAN   That was the winter when we all had the Asian flu.

And you tried to crawl off to your political meetings, and on top of that insisted you could manage the kids without help *and* run the house *and* hold down a job. *That* was a quarrel.

MARIANNE Then we gave it up. *(Pause)* It was fun while it lasted.

JOHAN Yes, I suppose it was.

MARIANNE We believed in humanity's future, anyway.

JOHAN It's always nice to have a belief, I grant you. Besides, we had the pleasure of annoying our parents, and that meant a lot. You weren't even-tempered in those days. Cute and hot-tempered. In fact, you were damned attractive as a socialist.

MARIANNE Aren't I now?

JOHAN What?

MARIANNE Damned attractive.

JOHAN Yes, of course you're attractive. Why?

MARIANNE I've also been thinking about it.

JOHAN Must it always be that two people who live together for a long time begin to tire of each other?

MARIANNE We haven't tired.

JOHAN Almost.

MARIANNE *(Indulgently)* We work too hard—that's what's so banal. And in the evenings we're too tired.

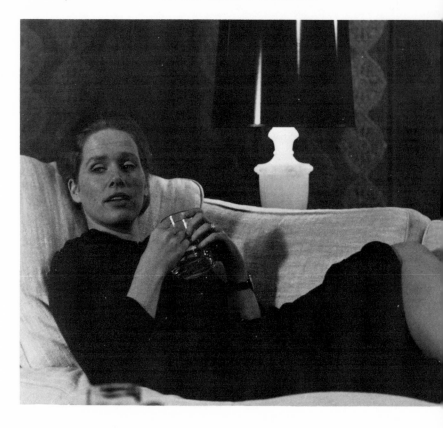

JOHAN   Marianne, that wasn't a reproach.

MARIANNE   I'm not so sure.

JOHAN   Word of honor.

MARIANNE   But we like each other in every way.

JOHAN   Not in that way. Not very much anyhow.

MARIANNE   Oh yes, we do.

JOHAN   It's just that our life together has become full of evasions and restrictions and refusals.

MARIANNE *(Hurt)*   I can't help it if I don't enjoy it as much as I used to. I can't help it. There's a perfectly natural explanation. You're not to accuse me and give me a bad conscience about this.

JOHAN *(Kind)*   You needn't get so upset!

MARIANNE   I think it's all right as it is. God knows it isn't passionate, but you can't expect everything. There are those who are much worse off than we are.

JOHAN   Without a doubt.

MARIANNE   Sex isn't everything. As a matter of fact.

JOHAN *(Laughing)*   Why, Marianne!

MARIANNE *(On the verge of tears)*   If you're not satisfied with my performance you'd better get yourself a mistress who is more imaginative and sexually exciting. I do my best, I'm sure.

JOHAN *(Sourly)*   There we have it.

MARIANNE   You've got that look again.

JOHAN   I haven't got any look.

MARIANNE   That look and that tone of voice. Whatever it is you're brooding about, come out with it.

JOHAN   It's no use. You lose your temper at whatever I say on this subject.

MARIANNE   No, I promise. I'm listening. Quite objectively.

JOHAN Sometimes I wonder why we complicate this problem so frightfully. This business of lovemaking is pretty elementary, after all. It was surely never meant to be a huge problem overshadowing everything else. It's all your mother's fault, if you ask me. Though you don't like my saying so.

MARIANNE I just think it's so damn superficial of you to talk like that.

JOHAN Don't be so sour, Marianne. I'm being kind.

MARIANNE All the same, you think it's my fault that we don't enjoy it any more.

JOHAN You said just now that you do your best.

MARIANNE Yes, indeed I do. I do, Johan.

JOHAN Can't you hear yourself how awful that sounds?

MARIANNE So you think I'm lying?

JOHAN No, for Christ's sake! No! No!

MARIANNE Then I don't understand.

JOHAN Let's drop this subject now and go to bed. It's late anyway.

MARIANNE Isn't that just like you. First you start a huge discussion and then, having got me all worked up, you yawn and say you're sleepy and want to go to bed.

JOHAN Marianne! *(Pause)* You suffer from devastatingly high standards. We've often joked about it. Sometimes we've quarreled about it too. But can't our poor sex life be spared your ambitions.

MARIANNE *(In tears)*   Why must you always wrangle with me on this particular point? First you abuse me for not trying, and then you abuse me because I exert myself.

JOHAN *(Gently)*   Now look what I've gone and done.

MARIANNE   Yes, haven't you. Can't you be nice and kind instead. It would help a lot more.

JOHAN   Yes. *(Giving up)* There, there, sweetheart, don't be upset. It was silly of me to bring all this up.

MARIANNE   Let me tell you this. You can talk too much about these things.

JOHAN *(Giving up)*   I suspect you're right.

MARIANNE   I know you're supposed to tell everything and not keep anything secret, but in this particular matter I think it's wrong.

JOHAN *(Who has heard this before)*   Yes, you're probably right.

MARIANNE *(Following up her advantage)*   There are things which must be allowed to live their life in a half-light, away from prying eyes.

JOHAN *(Total retreat)*   You think so?

MARIANNE   I'm quite convinced of it. We upset and hurt each other all to no purpose when we carry on like this. And all the barbs are still there when we get into bed. My God, it's like lying on a bed of nails.

JOHAN *(Laughing)*   Ha . . .

MARIANNE *(Suspicious)*   What are you laughing at?

JOHAN   The bed of nails.

MARIANNE *(More graciously)*   It's all very well for you to laugh.

JOHAN   Can't we go to bed now?

MARIANNE   You must admit you've been unusually stupid and cocky and tactless.

JOHAN   I apologize.

MARIANNE   Do you think I don't give you enough affection?

JOHAN   Affection takes time.

MARIANNE   Then you *don't* get enough.

JOHAN   *We* don't get enough. And don't give enough.

MARIANNE   That's why I wanted us to go away together this summer.

JOHAN   I don't think affection should be kept only for vacations.

MARIANNE *(Kissing him)*   You're kind anyway, even if you *are* an idiot.

JOHAN   Then it's lucky I'm married to you.

MARIANNE *(Kissing him)*   You have your great moments, but in-between you're horribly mediocre.

JOHAN   At our age tens of thousands of brain cells snuff out every day. And they're never replaced.

MARIANNE *(Kissing him)*   With you it must be ten times as many, you're so silly.

JOHAN   You're sweet even if you do scold and make a fuss. *(He kisses her and touches her breasts. She moves his hand gently away. He gives a short laugh, stands up, and yawns.* MARIANNE *smiles a little guiltily)* I'm nearly asleep.

MARIANNE   I'll just look in on the children.
(When she goes into the girls' room she sees that KARIN *is lying awake, silent and unmoving)* Why, Kajsa! Aren't you asleep?

KARIN   No.

MARIANNE   Why not?

KARIN   I'm afraid to sleep, I have such nasty dreams.

MARIANNE   What sort of dreams?

KARIN   Every time I go to sleep I dream there's a war.

MARIANNE   Would you like a glass of milk?

KARIN   Yes, please.
*(*MARIANNE *goes out into the kitchen and gets a glass of milk. When she comes back* KARIN *has fallen asleep. She puts the glass on the bedside table and tiptoes out of the room, leaving the door ajar.* JOHAN *is already lying in their big double bed. He is wearing glasses and reading. She too picks up a book, puts on her glasses, takes a sip of water, swallows a little pill, and snuggles down. Soon afterward* JOHAN *puts his light out.* MARIANNE *switches hers off too)*

JOHAN   Good night.

MARIANNE   Good night, darling.

JOHAN   Have you set the alarm?

MARIANNE   Yes, I actually remembered. *(Pause)* Johan! If you'd like to make love I . . .

JOHAN Thanks for the offer, but I'm nearly asleep. Good night, darling.

MARIANNE Good night. Sleep well.

THIRD SCENE
Paula

The house in the country. Late evening.

MARIANNE *has gone to bed and is almost asleep. When she hears the car drive up she is wide awake and immediately gay. She leaps out of bed and rushes downstairs in nothing but her nightie.* JOHAN *enters from the veranda and puts down his little bag.*

Before he has time to take his coat off, she flings her arms around his neck, hugs him, and gives him four loud kisses.

MARIANNE   Here already! You weren't coming until tomorrow. What a lovely surprise. Are you hungry? And me with my hair in curlers. How good of you to come this evening. The children are asleep, we went to bed early. There was nothing on TV and we thought it would be nice to have an early night. The girls and I have been dieting today. Would you like an omelet or a sandwich and some beer?

JOHAN   That sounds good.

MARIANNE   Or would you like a real meal? Shall I fry some eggs and bacon? Or heat some soup?

JOHAN   Sandwiches and beer are fine. While I think of it, I have a message from Peter and Katarina. They're going to call you up on Monday at the office.

MARIANNE   That's a long and nerve-racking business, poor things.

JOHAN   *Are* they getting divorced? It seems to me as if they don't know what they want to do.

MARIANNE   Do you think that's so strange? I've asked them to each get a lawyer, but they won't. Why not get undressed and I'll bring the tray up to the bedroom.

JOHAN   No, I'd rather sit in the kitchen.

MARIANNE   And here I've been worrying that you were angry with me.

JOHAN   Why should I be angry with you?

MARIANNE   You know quite well! I was beastly on the phone last night.

JOHAN   Oh, that! That was nothing.

MARIANNE   I called you right back, but you must have pulled the plug out.

JOHAN   I was pretty tired last night. I'd been out all day at the institute with that zombie from the ministry. You wonder sometimes who these idiots are who sit on the state money-bags and determine our weal and woe.

MARIANNE   I still think I was nasty to you last night. I really do.

JOHAN   Can't we just forget it?

MARIANNE   You *are* funny, you never finish talking about any-thing. I won't be long-winded, darling. All I want to say is that I think you're right. And I'm right too. In a different way. If you don't want to go out to dinner in a tuxedo, then that's your business. You're right there. On the other hand, I do think you could get yourself a new tuxedo.

JOHAN   I don't like tuxedos. I hate wearing a tuxedo. I think it's an idiotic get-up. I feel like a dressed-up chimpanzee in a tuxedo.

MARIANNE   Yes, I remember you said that. *(Laughs)* Well, let's not start quarreling again. I love you, even if you won't dress up in a tuxedo. It's not absolutely essential to our marriage.

JOHAN   It seemed like it last night.

MARIANNE   I told you I was wrong. God, I am getting hungry watching you eat. I'll simply have to have a sandwich. It can't be helped. I'm dizzy with hunger. I've lost over four pounds this last week. Does it show?

JOHAN   No.

MARIANNE   I feel it anyway, let me tell you. Sometimes everything seems utterly pointless. Why should we grudge ourselves all the good things in the world? Why can't we be big and fat and good-tempered? Just think how nice it would make us. Do you remember Aunt Miriam and Uncle David? They were perfect dears and got along so well together, and they were so *fat!* And every night they lay there in the big creaky double bed, holding hands and content with each other just as they were, fat and cheerful. Couldn't you and I be like Aunt Miriam and Uncle David and go around looking comfortable and safe? Shall I take my curlers out?

JOHAN   Don't mind me.

MARIANNE   Yes, I will. I know you don't like them. No, let's leave the washing up. Come on, darling, let's go to bed. You must be awfully tired and I'm a bit drowsy too, though I slept for a while before you came. What is it, Johan? Are you worried about something? Has something happened? What's wrong? Tell me what it is.

JOHAN   I came here this evening to tell you something. I've gone and fallen in love, you see. It's quite absurd and maybe it's all a goddamn mistake. It probably is a goddamn mistake. I met her during the convention in June. She was the interpreter and secretary. Actually, she's studying for her degree. She's going to teach Slavic languages. She's nothing much to look at. In fact, you'd undoubtedly think she was ugly. I have no idea what this will lead to. I have no idea about anything. I'm completely bewildered. Of course I'm pleased in one way. Though I have a hell of a bad conscience about you and the children. We've always got along well, haven't we? I mean, things haven't been any better or worse for us than for the average family. Say something, for Christ's sake.

MARIANNE   I don't know what to say.

JOHAN   I suppose you think it was wrong of me not to tell you about this before. But I didn't know how it would turn out. I thought: I'll soon get over it. It's just a passing phase. So I didn't want to worry you.

MARIANNE   It's so funny.

JOHAN   What's funny?

MARIANNE   That I haven't realized anything. That I haven't been suspicious or noticed anything. Everything has been as usual, better in fact. You've been so kind. And I've just gone around like a silly fool, blind and unsuspecting. God in heaven!

JOHAN   No, you haven't noticed anything. But then you never were very clear-sighted. Especially where our personal relations were concerned.

MARIANNE   What are we to do now then?

JOHAN I don't know.

MARIANNE Do you want a divorce? Are you going to marry
her? Anyway, why do you have to tell me about this tonight
of all times? Why the sudden hurry?

JOHAN We're going to Paris tomorrow afternoon.
(MARIANNE *looks at him in silence*) I want to get away from all
this. At any rate for a time. I was going down anyway in the
fall to see Grandin and his assistant. And Paula has a study
grant and was going to use it up this fall. I want to be with
her. I can't be without her. So we're leaving together tomorrow afternoon. (MARIANNE *looks at him in silence*) Now that
I'm talking to you, now that I'm at home, I'd prefer to scrap
the whole damn thing. I feel tired and scared. (MARIANNE
looks at him in silence) Nothing could be sillier or more com-
monplace and absurd than this. I know just what you're
thinking and I have no excuses to offer.

MARIANNE How can you know what I'm thinking?

JOHAN I'm trying not to have a bad conscience, but it's only
affectation. This is the way it *is*, Marianne. There's nothing
to be done about it. (MARIANNE *looks at him in silence*) We'd
better not talk. There's nothing sensible to say in any case.
You know the truth now and that's the main thing.

MARIANNE I know nothing. Let's go to bed. It's late. And I
suppose you're off early.

JOHAN I have a meeting at nine.

MARIANNE Then I suggest we go to bed. (*They go upstairs to the
bedroom.* MARIANNE *sits on the bed and watches* JOHAN *undress. He
is embarrassed by her gaze, and to make matters worse he has some
incriminating marks on his chest*) You have marks on your
chest.

JOHAN I know.

MARIANNE *(Smiling)* How indiscreet of you both.

JOHAN Do you know if my gray suit is here or in town? I've been hunting for it.

MARIANNE It's at the dry cleaners.

JOHAN What a nuisance.

MARIANNE I have the receipt if you'd like to call for it tomorrow.

JOHAN I won't have time. I'll be busy all day until three o'clock, and then we're off.

MARIANNE If you like, I'll drive in and pick it up for you. And I'll gladly do your packing. You're not very good at it.

JOHAN No thank you.

MARIANNE *(Smiling)* You're being silly.

JOHAN Yes, I am in fact rather conventional.

MARIANNE Otherwise I think you have all you need. There are clean shirts and underclothes here, so you can take those with you. Can't you travel in your jacket and flannel pants? They give you a nice youthful air.

JOHAN Yes, I suppose so.

MARIANNE How long will you be away?

JOHAN I don't know. It all depends.

MARIANNE What do you mean?

JOHAN   I have requested and been given six months' leave of absence. Before then I have about a month's work which I'm taking with me. So it will be seven or eight months at least.

MARIANNE *(Thunderstruck)*   Oh.

JOHAN   It's just as well to make a clean break.

MARIANNE   Do you suppose I'll still be here when you come back?

JOHAN   I don't give a damn.

MARIANNE   I see.

JOHAN   Do you know how long I've had this in mind? Can you guess? I don't mean about Paula, but about leaving you and the children and our home. Can you guess?

MARIANNE *(Looks at him in alarm)*   Don't tell me.

JOHAN   For four years I've wanted to get rid of you. Not that I didn't like you. You mustn't think that.

MARIANNE *(Drawing the sheet up to her face)*   No more now.

JOHAN   No, you're right. It's just empty words.

MARIANNE   What are you going to live on? I mean now, during your leave of absence. You'll have to pay an allowance to the children in any case.

JOHAN   Don't worry. I have enough to get by on.

MARIANNE   Then you must have income that I don't know of.

JOHAN   How right you are.

MARIANNE How is that possible?

JOHAN *(Beside himself)* Listen now, for Christ's sake, though it's no goddamn business of yours. For one thing I've sold the boat, and for another I've taken a loan, which Frid has been kind enough to put his name to. From the first of September the bank will pay one thousand six hundred kronor a month to you and the girls. For the time being. Then we'll make some other arrangement when I come home. You'd better talk to one of your lawyer colleagues at the office. I don't give a damn. Name your price. I'm not taking anything with me, except perhaps my books, if you have no objection. I'll just vanish, do you hear? Into thin air. I will pay all I reasonably can to support you and the children. My needs are nil. All that interests me is to take the step out of all this. Do you know what I'm most fed up with? All this fucking harping on what we're supposed to do, what we must do, what we must take into consideration. What your mother will think. What the children will say. How we had best arrange that dinner party and shouldn't we invite my father after all. We must go to the west coast. We must go to the mountains. We must go to St. Moritz. We must celebrate Christmas, Easter, Whitsun, birthdays, namedays, the whole fucking lot. I know I'm being unfair. I know that what I'm saying now is all goddamn nonsense. I know that we've had a good life. And actually I think I still love you. In fact, in one way I love you *more* now since I met Paula. But can you understand this bitterness? I don't know what to call it. This bitterness, I can't hit on any better word. No one can explain it to me for the simple reason that I have no one to talk to except Erik Broméus and he's intellectually illiterate, so he hasn't much to offer except his money, and there are worse things than that in this situation. No, I don't understand. I don't understand this thing I call bitterness, which has kept getting worse and worse.

MARIANNE Why haven't you said anything?

JOHAN   How can one talk about something which hasn't any words? How can one say that it's boring to make love although technically everything is perfect? How can I say that it's all I can do not to strike you when you sit there at the breakfast table all neat and tidy eating your boiled eggs? And the girls giving themselves airs in that silly spoiled way. Why have we indulged them so hysterically? Can you tell me that? I'm not blaming you, Marianne. Everything has just gone to pot. And no one knows why.

MARIANNE   I must have been doing wrong the whole time.

JOHAN   Stop that. It's an easy way out always to take the blame. It makes you feel strong and noble and generous and humble. You haven't done wrong and I haven't done wrong. It's no use trotting out guilty feelings and a bad conscience, though God knows my conscience is so bad it's nearly choking me. It's all sheer chance, a cruel coincidence. Why should you and I of all people be able to dodge the humiliations and the disasters? It's all perfectly logical. So why start talking about guilt and doing wrong.

MARIANNE   My poor darling.

JOHAN   I don't want your sympathy. Don't paw me. I think it's only affectation on my part. I mean this empty talk. I don't think for one minute I'm getting at the truth about us. As a matter of fact, I don't think there *is* any plain truth. It's just a lot of sores everywhere. And whichever way we turn and whatever we say, it hurts.

MARIANNE   Won't you change your mind and not go?

JOHAN   That's impossible.

MARIANNE   But if I plead with you.

JOHAN   It's no use, and it's only distressing.

MARIANNE   Can't you at least postpone the trip for a month or two? You're not giving me a chance. I think we could repair our marriage. I think we could find a new form for our life together. Perhaps Paula would understand me better than you do. I ought to meet her and talk to her. It's a mistake to cut everything off just when we're starting to be honest with each other. Can't we let the disaster sweep over us together? I mean, we're destroying so much by tearing down all we've built up. You must give me a chance, Johan. It's unkind of you just to present me with a *fait accompli*. You're putting me in a ridiculous and intolerable position. Surely you can see that.

JOHAN   I know just what you mean: What are our parents going to say? What will my sister think, what will our friends think? Jesus Christ, how tongues are going to wag! How will it affect the girls, and what will their school friends' mothers think? And what about the dinner parties we're invited to in September and October. And what are you going to say to Katarina and Peter? To hell with all that! I intend to behave like a cad, and what a relief!

MARIANNE   That wasn't what I meant.

JOHAN   Oh, what did you mean?

MARIANNE   *(Softly)*   Nothing. *(They've gotten into the big double bed and put out the light. Neither can get to sleep. They lie for a long time silent and unmoving, deeply distressed. There is complete silence around them)* I forgot to set the alarm. What time do you have to get up?

JOHAN   Set it for five thirty, will you. I must do some packing too. I have to be at the institute at nine for a conference.

MARIANNE   I've been meaning to get another alarm clock. This one is loud enough to wake the dead. It's not terribly reliable either. There, it's set for five thirty. Anyway, I usually wake up without an alarm. Don't worry. *(Suddenly)* I want you to tell me about Paula.

JOHAN   What's the point of that?

MARIANNE   Please.

JOHAN   Why do you want to torment yourself?

MARIANNE   It's not self-torment. I want to know what she's like. It's much worse to go around trying to picture someone who has no outlines. Do you have a photo of her? You must.

JOHAN   Please, Marianne, can't we be spared?

MARIANNE   Do, I beg you. Can't you help me with this?

JOHAN   Well, let it be on your own head. Where's my wallet? Oh yes, in my coat pocket. Here are two photos. One was taken two years ago, when she was on vacation down by the Black Sea. The other's a passport photo taken a couple of weeks ago. It's a good likeness, I think.

MARIANNE   She has a nice figure. Lovely breasts, it seems. Are they?

JOHAN   Yes, she has lovely breasts.

MARIANNE   Does she dye her hair? It looks like it, I mean.

JOHAN   It hadn't occurred to me, but it's possible.

MARIANNE   She has a nice smile. How old is she?

JOHAN   Twenty-three. She hasn't been very lucky in love. She's been engaged twice and I think in that particular respect she's made a muddle of her life with all kinds of men.

MARIANNE Does that upset you?

JOHAN I'll say it does. Her outspokenness can sometimes be
rather unpleasant. I would prefer not to know anything, but
she insists on giving me the details of her erotic past. It's
rather trying, since I suffer from retrospective jealousy. She
has no illusions. She says that she has no great hopes for the
two of us. She says she knows that I'll go back to you, that
she doesn't have a chance against you. Sometimes it sounds
like lines from a badly written old play that one has seen far
too often. She has a compulsion to safeguard herself against
every form of failure. It makes her rather sympathetic.
There's something childish about her altogether, despite her
twenty-three years and her intelligence and general capabil-
ity. She's horribly jealous, but then so am I, so in that we're
alike. She's terribly afraid of you, and that I can understand.
But she's also afraid of my secretary and of other women
whom she knows I associate with. She's unsure of herself in
many ways. I try to help her all I can. It's all pretty strange
and bewildering.

MARIANNE Are you good together in bed?

JOHAN At first it was dreadful. I suppose it was my fault too.
I'm not really used to it. I mean with other women, and you
and I have spoiled each other. I couldn't do a thing. But she
said that no one had ever been so kind and tender toward
her. I wanted to break the whole thing off, although I was
in love with her. You see, I realized that if I couldn't have
sex with her, the whole affair was doomed. But she got in
an awful state when I wanted to end it all. I was afraid she
would hurt herself. Then we were out of town for a week.

MARIANNE Did you go away together?

JOHAN Yes. You remember I gave some lectures in Copenhagen in April.

MARIANNE   Oh, it was then. In April.

JOHAN   We lived it up in the evenings and behaved like pigs.
We got mixed up in drunken brawls and were kicked out of
the hotel. You remember I told you I had changed my hotel
because the traffic was so noisy. We ended up in a squalid
little place on a back street, and suddenly we clicked and
made love day and night. She said that it had never been so
good for her before. I felt terrifically high, of course. I know
what you're thinking, Marianne, and it's true. You and I
also had much better times together after that Copenhagen
trip.

MARIANNE   Did you tell Paula that?

JOHAN   No, I didn't dare. I told her that you and I stopped
sleeping together long ago. I said I was impotent. It wasn't
exactly true, but I had been impotent with her, so I might
just as well pretend I was impotent with you too. But the
trouble with Paula is that she has the devil of an intuition.
Or else I'm a bad liar. She always looks right at me when I'm
not telling the truth. She has an alarming gift for seeing
through me. Which is good for me, to be sure. It teaches me
a lesson.

MARIANNE   Yes, I've always been so unsuspecting.

JOHAN   Not *only* unsuspecting. Both you and I have escaped
into a state of existence that has been hermetically sealed.
Everything has been neatly arranged, all cracks have been
stopped up, it has all gone like clockwork. We have died
from lack of oxygen.

MARIANNE   *(Smiling)*   And now you mean that along comes
your little Paula and awakens you to a new life.

JOHAN   I don't have much self-knowledge and I understand
very little of reality in spite of having read a lot of books. But

something tells me that this catastrophe is a chance in a million for both you and me.

MARIANNE   Is it Paula who has put such nonsense into your head? Just how naïve can you get?

JOHAN   We can do without taunts and sarcastic remarks in this conversation.

MARIANNE   You're right. I'm sorry.

JOHAN   I'm trying, do you hear? I'm trying to be as honest as I can. It isn't easy. We've never talked about these things. Is it any wonder we're naïve and silly and uncertain? How else could it be? This affair with Paula is a catastrophe. Both for you and me. I've tried to break free time and again, but it's been impossible. She won't let me go, and in one way I'm —obsessed by her. It sounds so damn melodramatic to say you're "obsessed" by anyone, but it's the only adequate word. At first I resisted but now I let everything go to hell. And I'm quite content to have it that way.

MARIANNE   All I ask is that you postpone the trip.

JOHAN   Paula would never agree to put it off and I feel the same way. I've made up my mind.

MARIANNE   Can't I meet her?

JOHAN   What's the use? Besides, she won't hear you spoken of. I hardly dare to mention your name.

MARIANNE   You *are* in a spot.

JOHAN   It depends how you look at it. Paula and I get along well together. She's cheerful and kind and tender. We always have lots to talk about. In-between we have the most awful fights. But I'm beginning to wonder if it isn't pretty salutary. All my life I've been so goddamn well-behaved and sensible and balanced and cautious. I don't know. I don't know anything.

MARIANNE   Come and lie beside me. I want you to make love to me. You can do that anyway. I mean for old times' sake. *(She switches off the bedside lamp. At the window it is already dawn. They have sex. Very soon she has a violent orgasm. Then she begins to weep. She turns on her side, hides her face in her hands, and sobs. After a little while she calms down, embraces her husband ardently but gently, and kisses him several times. They look at each other tenderly and in despair)* Lie here now in my arms and let's sleep. We're both awfully tired.

JOHAN   I don't think I can sleep. The best thing would be to have some coffee and pack and leave at once.

MARIANNE   No, lie down and close your eyes. You'll go to sleep, you'll see. We need some sleep both of us. It will be a strenuous day tomorrow.

JOHAN   I'm so goddamn ashamed.

MARIANNE   Let's wait with all that. It's only you and me now. We have these few hours to ourselves. Just you and me.
(They fall asleep at last in each other's arms. MARIANNE *wakes up with a start. Knowledge floods over her. At first she lies quite still in order to withstand the attack better, but it just increases in violence. It is easier if she moves. She turns carefully, frees herself from her husband's embrace, and reaches out her hand to shut off the alarm clock. There are still a few minutes to go before five thirty.* JOHAN *is sound asleep but has a worried expression. She props her head in her hand and regards him for a long time while the alarm clock ticks the seconds away behind her ear.*

Then the time is up and she touches him gently. He awakes instantly. Reaching out his arm he draws her to him in a gesture of helpless despair. She submits but is stiff and unwilling. They lie like this for a moment or two, then he releases her and sits up resolutely. He gets out of bed, goes into the bathroom, and begins to shave with the electric razor. MARIANNE *goes first to the toilet and has a pee, sits for a few moments as though paralyzed, feeling that she weighs about two tons, then goes to the sink and begins to wash.* JOHAN *has a long, thorough shower, then they stand there together, two mute naked strangers, drying themselves with their luxurious colored bathtowels.* MARIANNE *combs and brushes her long hair.* JOHAN *goes back to the bedroom and begins to get dressed)*

MARIANNE   Shall we pack now or have breakfast first? Would you like tea or coffee, by the way?

JOHAN   Oh, you decide. Tea, please. (MARIANNE *gets a suitcase down from a closet.* JOHAN *takes his traveling clothes—jacket and flannel pants—out of another and finishes dressing.* MARIANNE *begins to pack fussily.* JOHAN *goes into the bathroom, combs his hair and brushes his teeth, and comes back with the nail scissors)* Help me, please. I've a split nail and can't manage it.
(MARIANNE *gets her glasses and leads him over to the window. She starts clipping carefully)*

MARIANNE   You're biting your cuticles again.

JOHAN   Do you know what has become of Speer's memoirs? I'm sure I left the book on the bedside table.

MARIANNE   I thought you'd finished it, so I lent it to Mother.

JOHAN   Oh. Decent of you. Ow! Christ!

MARIANNE   I must cut down here. You've broken the nail. It's bleeding slightly, I'll have to put on a bandaid. What do you *do* to your nails?

JOHAN   Thank you, that's fine.

MARIANNE   Shall I pack the shaver, or will you take the one you have in town?

JOHAN   I have to go up to the apartment anyway to fetch some things, so you can leave it.

MARIANNE   Do you want the receipt for the dry cleaners?

JOHAN   I might as well take it, in case I have time. Which cleaners is it?

MARIANNE   The one in Storgatan, almost opposite the church.

JOHAN   Oh, I know. I'm not lugging those heavy shoes with me, if that's what you think.

MARIANNE   They might come in handy in the winter. Which pajamas are you taking?

JOHAN   Look, get out of here and make breakfast, while I finish packing.

MARIANNE   Does it bother you my helping you to pack?

JOHAN   I can't deny that I think it's indecent, though I don't know why. *(They both laugh helplessly.* MARIANNE *pulls on a shabby old pair of slacks and a large sweater.* JOHAN *goes on stubbornly packing.* MARIANNE *stands watching him with her arms crossed. After a strained silence* JOHAN *loses his temper)* What are you gaping at?

MARIANNE   Nothing. I'm sorry. *(She turns on her heel and goes out, leaving* JOHAN *to his packing. His irritation grows. When he tries to shut the suitcase and fails, he snatches out the winter shoes and hurls them across the floor.* MARIANNE *is busy with the breakfast, laying the kitchen table, boiling eggs, making tea and toast.* JOHAN *goes past with the suitcase on his way out to the car. He opens the trunk and tosses it in. Before* MARIANNE *can stop them, the tears are running down her cheeks, but she sniffles and blows her nose and pulls herself together. They sit down to breakfast, passing things to each other with ingrained routine.* MARIANNE *has forgotten to salt the eggs)* What shall I do with your mail?

JOHAN I'll write and tell you my address. Then you can send important letters on, if you don't mind. And if you'd be good enough to pay bills and so on in the usual way.

MARIANNE Another thing. The plumber was supposed to come and repair the bathroom before we move back to town. Have you spoken to him, or shall I call him up? You said you'd get in touch with him. I mean, if you've forgotten it in all the muddle, I could see to it that he comes and gets those jobs done at last.

JOHAN I've phoned him dozens of times, but he's never there. So I have *not* forgotten, as you seem to think.

MARIANNE What are you going to do with your car while you're away? Will you keep it in the garage?

JOHAN I've asked Paula's sister to look after it. There's no point in its standing idle, and she has just moved out of town.

MARIANNE I see.

JOHAN But if you wouldn't mind canceling my appointment with the dentist. I'm sure to forget.

MARIANNE One thing that's rather a problem: What are we going to do about your father's birthday on Friday? He asked us to dinner, you know. I'd be very grateful if you'd call him and explain things. Will you do that, please?

JOHAN That's about the worst thing of all. Perhaps I can write to him.

MARIANNE As long as you don't forget.

JOHAN   It's damned awkward about our parents. It feels so humiliating in some way. What can one say?

MARIANNE   Another thing. What do you want me to say to Mrs. Andersson?

JOHAN   Oh, shit! I couldn't care less what the cleaning woman thinks.

MARIANNE   Why are you so angry? (JOHAN *mutters something inaudible*) She has cleaned for us for ten years and knows us well and is indispensable and awfully loyal.

JOHAN   Uh. *(Pause)* Oh, you might just as well know. She caught Paula and me red-handed one morning. I didn't know you and she had changed the day, and there she was suddenly in the bedroom. A *very* awkward moment. *(Pause)* That was about a month ago. My car had broken down and we'd had dinner at a place not far away, and I thought it wouldn't matter so much if we spent the night at the apartment. I went out to the old girl in the kitchen and told her to keep her trap shut. She was practically drooling with excitement and moral indignation and loyalty to you. Then she fussed around and got breakfast for us, treating Paula more or less like the innocent victim of my brutal lusts. In the end I found myself bribing her with an extra thirty kronor. Why don't you say something?

MARIANNE   Then I needn't mention the matter to Mrs. Andersson. That's a relief.
(She gets up from the table and begins to clear. There is a clatter of dishes. Then she stands stock-still over by the sink, her head drooping and her breath coming in long, painful gasps)

JOHAN   *(Kindly)*   What is it, Marianne?

MARIANNE   Oh, it will pass. *(Then it's time for him to go. They stand facing each other in the hall. He puts on his overcoat)*

What do you want me to tell the children?

JOHAN   Tell them anything you like.

MARIANNE   Shall I tell them you've fallen in love with another woman and have cleared out and left us?

JOHAN   I don't think you could put it better. It also has the advantage of being true. I don't look for understanding from that quarter.

MARIANNE   Karin is going to take it badly. She's so attached to you right now. She never stops talking about you.

JOHAN   Don't paw me. It hurts enough as it is. I must go now. I want to try to get into town before the morning traffic jam. So long, Marianne, take care of yourself.

MARIANNE   So long.
(They stand there stiff, scared, and uncertain. He bends down to kiss her on the lips but she turns her face away. He gives a laugh)

JOHAN   I may be home in a week.

MARIANNE   If only you were. We'd make a fresh start in every way. We'd dig up all routine and negligence. We'd talk over the past. We'd try to find where we've gone wrong. You'd never hear any accusations. I promise you. It's all so unreal. I don't know what to do about it. You're shutting me out. I think any solution at all would be better than this. Can't you promise to come back? Then I'd know *something*. I mean, you can't just leave me without any hope. It's not fair. Even if you have no intention of returning, you could at least *say* you're coming home again.

JOHAN   I must go now, Marianne.
(He shakes his head and looks at her unseeing. Then he walks out the door. She stands still, the door closes. Through the window she sees him get into the car. After a couple of attempts it starts reluctantly and glides out of the gate and down the hill, turning to the right and disappearing behind the rise. MARIANNE *stands for a long time rooted to the ground, as if every movement from now on were going to cost her the most terrible effort. At last she drags herself out to the kitchen and starts to do the washing-up. She turns the radio on. Suddenly she breaks off and goes into the girls' bedroom. Silence and deep sleep prevail. She sits down for a moment and looks at their sleeping faces)*

MARIANNE   *(To herself)*   I don't understand. No, I don't understand. *(Then she gets an idea. She goes to the telephone and dials a number. After a time someone answers)* Hello, Fredrik, it's Marianne. Sorry to wake you. Is Birgit there? No, it doesn't matter. Let her sleep. How are things? Oh, you like puttering around alone at this hour. No, I won't keep you long. No, it's cloudy here. Oh, how nice for you. Well, I wanted to talk to you about something. No, I just wanted someone

to talk to. You and Birgit *are* our friends. I must have . . .
I must . . . it's all so unreal, Fredrik. You see—*(Pause)*—You
see, it's like this. I'm about to burst into tears any moment
and then I'll just go on crying, and I don't *want* to cry
because that will only make it worse. You see, Johan has
fallen in love with another woman. Her name's Paula, and
they're going off to Paris today. Can't you talk to Johan and
ask him to wait a bit? He needn't rush off headlong like that.
What? You've already talked to him? Oh, I see. I see. So you
and Birgit have known all along. *You've known the whole time
and not said a word to me?* What a filthy, rotten way to behave.
How could you be so goddamn disloyal to me? I don't care
what you say. And all the times we've met and talked and

you have known and never said anything. *(In a fury) Christ!* Jesus Christ! Fucking nice friends you are! You can go to hell with your explanations. Just how many people have known of this? Oh, quite a number. I'm glad to know.

(She flings the phone down. When it rings she doesn't answer. She bites her hand to stop herself from screaming)

FOURTH SCENE
The Vale of Tears

CHARACTERS

MARIANNE

JOHAN

An evening in September a year later. The doorbell rings. MARIANNE, *who has been busy in the kitchen preparing a dinner for two, goes to open the door after a quick check-up in front of the mirror.*

JOHAN Hello.

MARIANNE Hello. Come in!

JOHAN Sorry if I'm late. I had trouble with the car. It wouldn't start. *(Kisses her on the cheek)* How pretty you are. And what a nice dress.

MARIANNE I'm glad you like it. I bought it a couple of days ago but regretted it afterwards. I didn't think it suited me. And it suddenly seemed much too red.

JOHAN It suits you admirably, I must say.

MARIANNE Do come in, Johan. I feel nervous standing here in the hall, making polite conversation.

JOHAN I'm nervous too. I haven't been able to settle down to anything all day. It's ridiculous, really. But I haven't seen you for quite a long time. Over six months.

MARIANNE How was it that you suddenly . . . ?

JOHAN Paula's in London for a week.

MARIANNE Oh, I see. Oh. Would you like a drink?

JOHAN Yes, please, I'd love a whisky. Straight. It settles the
stomach. I mean, it calms you down.

MARIANNE Have you taken to drinking whisky?

JOHAN Yes, just imagine.

MARIANNE I asked Aunt Berit to take charge of the girls for
tonight. So they're staying with her until the day after tomorrow. The delight is mutual. They're going to the theater
this evening, and tomorrow they have a holiday from school
and are going to the country.

JOHAN How practical. I mean, it would have been pretty
rough going to meet the children too. How are they?

MARIANNE You needn't ask after them out of politeness. But
we'll write down their birthdays in your diary, so that you
don't forget them again as you did this year. I bought them
each a present from you, but they saw through me. And that
wasn't very nice. Couldn't you take them out to dinner
sometimes? Or to the movies? It's pretty awful the way you
never get in touch with them. They hardly ever mention
you nowadays.

JOHAN That's understandable.

MARIANNE Why can't Paula let you see us without raising
Cain for days on end . . . ?

JOHAN If we're meeting just to give you the chance of moral-
izing, I'd better go at once.

MARIANNE You've said yourself that Paula is so jealous that you can't see either me or the children without there being a godawful fight.

JOHAN   What do you expect me to do about it?

MARIANNE   Are you so darn yellow that you can't tell her what *you* want to do? Are you so afraid of her making a scene that you let her boss you around?

JOHAN *(Wearily)*   Yes.

MARIANNE   I'm sorry.

JOHAN   It doesn't matter. I realize you think the situation is absurd. But don't scold me. It's no use.

MARIANNE   Would you like some more whisky?

JOHAN   Yes, please.

MARIANNE   How are things otherwise?

JOHAN   Oh, much the same. What about you?

MARIANNE   I can't complain. It might be worse.

JOHAN   I suppose it was silly of me to call up and suggest we meet. There's nothing we can talk about without hurting each other.

MARIANNE   Then I have an excellent suggestion. Let's have dinner. Undoubtedly we're both ravenous and that's why we're so touchy. Don't you think so?

JOHAN   A good idea.
    (As they stand up he puts his arms round her and kisses her on the lips. She submits with a slight protest. Then they look at each other and smile suddenly)

MARIANNE   You look a fright with that haircut. And you've put on weight, I think.

JOHAN   I must admit you really turn me on when we're close together like this. What are we going to do about it?

MARIANNE   Let's have dinner first. Then we'll see.

JOHAN   Have you bought a new dinner service?

MARIANNE   It's family stuff. Dear old Aunt Elsa died six months ago and left me a lot of household things for some obscure reason. She was always under the impression that I was so domestic. Most of it is unusable, but the china is nice. You're only getting a casserole, and wine and cheese. I haven't had time to produce anything fancier. But you usually like my cooking.

JOHAN It smells wonderful. *(Helping himself)* Have you heard that Martin is going to marry again?

MARIANNE My dear, I ran into them in town. They were terribly embarrassed and began to stammer and make excuses for not having called me up or anything the whole year. I felt quite sorry for them.

JOHAN Anyway, this new one he's got hold of is a flighty little piece. Though she's said to have money.

MARIANNE As a matter of fact I've heard just the opposite. Her father's firm went bankrupt not long ago.

JOHAN   Then poor old Martin has slipped up again.

MARIANNE   Isn't he one of your closest friends?

JOHAN   Not exactly. Why?

MARIANNE   You sound so smug.

JOHAN   A wise man has said that in our friends' misfortunes there is always something that doesn't entirely displease us. Skoal, Marianne. This is a very good wine.

MARIANNE   My dear, it's nothing very special. Just a rather cheap claret. But it *is* good.

JOHAN   I don't mind telling you that things are going pretty well for me just now. I've been offered a chair at a university in Cleveland for three years. It's a splendid chance, both career-wise and financially. After all, it's over there that things happen in our field. And I'd be more than glad to emigrate, either temporarily or for good. There's nothing to keep me here. I'm fed up with the academic duck-pond. Besides, I have no desire to let myself be fleeced to the bone. So I leave in the spring, if all goes well.

MARIANNE   Congratulations.

JOHAN   And now for the unspoken question: Are you taking Paula with you to America? And the answer is no. Call it running away, if you like. Okay, I'm decamping. I've had just about enough. Paula has been good for me. She has taught me a few things about myself which I'm glad to know. But there's a limit. To be quite frank, I'm pretty tired of her. I suppose you think it's disloyal of me to sit here running Paula down. But she forfeited my loyalty long ago. I'm fed up with her. With her emotional storms and scenes and tears and hysterics, then making it all up and saying how much she loves me. *(Checking himself)* I'll tell you this,

Marianne. The best thing about Paula was that she taught me to shout and brawl. It was even permissible to strike her. I wasn't aware that I had any feelings at all. If I were to tell you . . . you'd think I was lying. Sometimes I thought I was mixed up in a grotesque play, in which I was both actor and audience. Our fights used to go on for days and nights on end, until we collapsed from sheer exhaustion.

MARIANNE   Would you like another helping?

JOHAN   Thanks, I haven't quite finished this. It's simply delicious. And I'm talking your ear off. But it puts you in such a terribly good mood. I've felt on top of the world ever since I was offered that professorship.

MARIANNE *(Quietly)*   In that case perhaps we could discuss the divorce. I mean, if you're going to be away for several years it would be better to clinch the matter before you go. Don't you think?

JOHAN   You should do as you see fit.

MARIANNE   Then I suggest that we do get a divorce. One never knows what may happen. I might want to remarry. And it would be awfully complicated if you're in America.

JOHAN   Is something up?

MARIANNE   That made you curious, didn't it?

JOHAN   Look here, Marianne! Suppose you tell me something about yourself. And not just let me rattle on.

MARIANNE   Would you like some more wine?

JOHAN   No thanks. It has already gone to my head. No more of anything. Well, perhaps a little cheese. No, no, we don't need fresh plates. What sort of cheese is this? It looks tasty.

MARIANNE It's a Bel Paese. Try it.

JOHAN Delicious. But don't think you're wriggling out of it. How are things, Marianne? Judging by your appearance, your hairdo, your dress, your figure, and your general amiability, they must be pretty good. What I'm most anxious to know, of course, is whether you have a lover.

MARIANNE I'll make the coffee. You'd like some, wouldn't you?
(She goes around the table and, taking his head in both hands, bends down and kisses him on the lips. He lends a hand clearing the table. While MARIANNE *is making the coffee* JOHAN *wanders about rather restlessly. He stops in a doorway and looks in)*

JOHAN You've changed things around, I see.

MARIANNE Any objections?

JOHAN Oh, none at all.

MARIANNE I've moved into your study.

JOHAN And what have you done with my things?

MARIANNE *(Gaily)* They're in the storage and I'm paying for it. I decided finally that I had a right to a workroom of my own. So I bought some furniture and put up new curtains and my own pictures which there wasn't room for here in the old days and which you didn't like. Was that tactless, perhaps? Do you think I should have waited until the divorce was over? Should I have observed a year of mourning? Oh, and I've also changed the telephone, so it's in my name now.

JOHAN Oh, that's good.

MARIANNE You're a tiny bit bitter about something all the same.

JOHAN   By no means. I think you did right.

MARIANNE   Thank you. Before, I always had to sit and work at the writing desk in the bedroom when I brought work home. It was rather inconvenient. But all that mattered then was that you had a proper study where you were not disturbed by the children. Oh, and I've taken away the double bed.

JOHAN   What was the point of that?

MARIANNE   I nearly went crazy sleeping in one corner of a huge bed. So it's now a little more chaste here, as you see.

JOHAN   And what about your lover? Where do you house him?

MARIANNE   For the time being I think it's better for us to meet at his place.

JOHAN   You mean because of the girls?

MARIANNE *(With a smile)*   No, silly. They're always after me to get married again.

JOHAN   Well, I'll be damned.

MARIANNE   Would you like a brandy or something?

JOHAN   No thanks. This is a place fit for human beings to live in anyway.

MARIANNE *(Smiling)*   You live out of town, don't you?

JOHAN   We live in a concrete hutch consisting of three rooms. On the tenth floor. With a view of another concrete hut. At the downstairs entrance drunken thirteen-year-olds stagger about. They amuse themselves by knocking down the old people. The building has cracks everywhere. The windows fit so badly that the curtains flutter in the draught. For two whole weeks not long ago I had to get every drop of water from a hydrant. None of the toilets worked. If possible, people avoid the subway after eight in the evening. In the middle of it all is something which a demented architect has called the piazza. Not that I'm complaining. In fact I think it's interesting, since what it most resembles is my idea of hell.

MARIANNE   I didn't know you believed in hell.

JOHAN   Hell is a place where no one believes in solutions any more. But Paula likes it out there. She says it all fits in with her picture of the world. And that it feels safe. I don't really care where I live. To me every domicile is only temporary. You must have your security inside yourself.

MARIANNE   Do *you?*

JOHAN   I didn't, as long as I was living here at home. Everything around us then was so confoundedly important. We were forced to make a ritual of security.

MARIANNE   I don't know what you mean.

JOHAN   All security was anchored in the things outside ourselves. Our possessions, our country house, the apartment, our friends, our income, food, holidays, parents.

MARIANNE   *(Anxiously)*   Why did we stop showing each other affection, Johan? Why did we hardly ever kiss? Why did we only caress one another when we had sex? Why did we cuddle the children so little?

JOHAN   Do you know what my security looks like? I'll tell you. I think this way: Loneliness is absolute. It's an illusion to imagine anything else. Be aware of it. And try to act accordingly. Don't expect anything but trouble. If something nice happens, all the better. Don't think you can ever do away with loneliness. It is absolute. You can invent fellowship on different levels, but it will still only be a fiction about religion, politics, love, art, and so on. The loneliness is nonetheless complete. What's so treacherous is that sometime you may be struck by an idea of fellowship. Bear in mind that it's an illusion. Then you won't be so disappointed afterwards, when everything goes back to normal. You must live with the realization of absolute loneliness. Then you will stop complaining, then you will stop moaning. In fact, then you're pretty safe and are learning to accept with a certain satisfaction how pointless it all is. By that I don't mean that you should settle down resignedly. I think you should carry on as long as you can. If only because it's better for you to do your best than to give up.

MARIANNE   I wish I were as certain as you.

JOHAN   It's nothing but words. You put it into words so as to placate the great emptiness. It's funny, come to think of it. Has it ever struck you that emptiness hurts? You'd think it might make you dizzy or give you mental nausea. But my emptiness hurts physically. It stings like a burn. Or like when you were little and had been crying and the whole inside of your body ached. I'm astonished sometimes at Paula's tremendous political faith. It's both true and sincere and she's incessantly active within her group. Her conviction answers her questions and fills the emptiness. I wish I could live as she does. I really mean that, without any sarcasm. *(Leaning forward)* Why are you sneering? Do you think I'm talking rubbish? I think so too as a matter of fact. But I don't care.

MARIANNE   I don't know what you're talking about. It seems so theoretical. I don't know why. Perhaps because I never talk about such big matters. I think I move on another plane.

JOHAN *(Roughly)* A more select plane, oh. A special plane reserved for women with a privileged emotional life and a happier, more mundane adjustment to the mysteries of life. Paula too likes to change herself into a priestess of life. It's always when she has read a new book by some fancy preacher of the new women's gospel.

MARIANNE I remember you always talked and talked. I used to like it, though I hardly ever took any notice of what you said when you held forth at your worst. It sounds as if somewhere you were disappointed.

JOHAN *(Quietly)* That's what you think.

MARIANNE *(Gently)* I want you to know that I'm nearly always thinking of you and wondering if you're all right or whether you're lonely and afraid. Every day, several times a day, I wonder where I went wrong. What I did to cause the breach between us. I know it's a childish way of thinking, but there you are. Sometimes I seem to have got hold of the solution, then it slips through my fingers.

JOHAN *(Sarcastically)* Why don't you go to a psychiatrist?

MARIANNE I do go to a doctor who has also had psychiatric training, and we have a couple of talks a week. Sometimes we meet privately.

JOHAN Is *he* your lover?

MARIANNE We've gone to bed together a couple of times but it was a dead loss. So we gave up the attempt and devoted ourselves to my interesting mental life instead.

JOHAN And where has that got you?

MARIANNE Nowhere. I'm trying hard to learn to talk. Oh yes, and I got rid of your furniture and moved into your study.

If you only knew what a bad conscience I had!—while at the same time feeling awfully daring.

JOHAN   That was one result anyway. *(Yawns)*

MARIANNE   What a huge yawn. Are you tired?

JOHAN   It's just the wine. I'm sorry. And I don't sleep terribly well. That added to the tension, I suppose.

MARIANNE   If you'd like to go home, don't mind me.

JOHAN   Oh, don't make such a thing of it.

MARIANNE   You can lie down and have a nap if you like. I'll wake you in an hour.

JOHAN *(Smiling)*   What a fuss about that one wretched yawn. I don't *want* to lie down. Please tell me about your explorations inside yourself instead. That's much more interesting. I promise you.

MARIANNE   There's not really very much to tell. Though something funny did strike me. But I haven't spoken to the doctor about it because it only occurred to me last night.

JOHAN *(Not very interested)*   Oh, that sounds exciting.

MARIANNE   The doctor said I should write down whatever came into my head. It didn't matter how irrelevant. Anything at all. Dreams, memories, thoughts. There's nothing much so far. It's hard to write when you're not used to it. It sounds so stilted and you can't find the right words and you think how silly it all is.

JOHAN *(Politely)*   Won't you read me what you wrote last night? I'd like very much to hear it.

MARIANNE   Would you really? Are you sure? I'll go and get the book. I wrote for several hours and didn't get to sleep till about three o'clock. I looked a fright this morning and thought it *would* be today, just when I was going to see you after so long.
(During the foregoing she has been into her workroom and found the notebook, thick with black oilcloth covers. She comes back, cheerfully excited and smiling. She sits down and lights a reading lamp)

JOHAN   You really are fabulously pretty.

MARIANNE   Now don't start paying compliments. You must take an interest in my soul instead. Sit down, please. *(But* JOHAN *has gone up to her and embraced her. He gives her a long ardent kiss on the lips. She sits quite still, her face turned up and her eyes closed, and lets him kiss her. When he puts his hand on her breast she twists aside and pushes it away)* No, don't. Sit down and be good and I'll read to you instead.

JOHAN *(With a smile)*   One good thing needn't exclude another.

MARIANNE   I've been thinking about that the whole time. What would it matter if we made love this evening? I've been longing for it and have worked myself up. But then I thought—what about afterwards? I mean after you've gone. I'd be left longing for you again. And I don't want that. I'm in love with you, Johan. Don't you see? Sometimes I hate you for what you've done to me. And sometimes I don't think of you for several hours at a stretch. It's lovely. Oh no. I have everything I could want. I have friends and even lovers. I have my children and I hold down a good job and like my work. No one need feel sorry for me. But I'm bound to you. I can't think why. Maybe I'm a perverted masochist or else I'm just the faithful type who forms only one attachment in life. I don't know. It's so difficult, Johan. I don't want to live with anyone else. Other men bore me. I'm not saying this to give you a bad conscience or to blackmail you emotionally. I'm only telling you how it is. That's why I just can't bear it if you start kissing me and making love to me. Because then all my defenses break down. I can't explain it in any other way. And then it's so lonely again after you've gone. When I keep you at a distance like this it's all right. In fact, it's awfully nice. But don't let's fondle each other. Because then it's hopeless after you've gone.

JOHAN   I'm still in love with you. You know that.

MARIANNE   Why do you say that when it's not true?

JOHAN   Why should my feelings for you have changed? Do you imagine I haven't longed to come back to you nearly every day during this time? We had a good life together. We were always friends, we had fun together. If we feel like making love now, why shouldn't we? It only shows we still long for one another. Marianne! Why the mental reservations? Why think about how it's going to feel tomorrow? Isn't that being very silly?

(MARIANNE *lets him kiss her several times. He fondles her more and more passionately. The diary falls to the floor. He draws her down to him and starts unbuttoning her blouse. Then she breaks free and sits up, smoothing her hair and buttoning up her blouse. She shakes her head*)

MARIANNE   No, I don't want to. No! No, I don't *want* to. I don't want to moon about here, pining and weeping and longing. Please understand. Things really are the way I say. There's nothing sillier than this. If you persist, you might just as well go. I mean it, Johan. I don't want us to make love. I really don't. Please try to understand!

JOHAN   I'll try to understand although I don't. So I'll sit down here and you can give me a brandy and some more coffee. Then we'll devote ourselves to reading aloud instead and then I'll go home at a respectable hour and call Paula in London and tell her I've been to the theater.
(MARIANNE, *distressed, pats his cheek. They are embarrassed and upset. She gets the brandy and he pours himself more coffee. He takes out his pipe and fills it.* MARIANNE *puts on her reading glasses. They toast each other jokingly.* MARIANNE *has a lump in her throat but manages to control herself.* JOHAN *lights his pipe with several matches.* MARIANNE *turns the pages of the notebook*)

MARIANNE   I feel like an awful fool now. I want to run away and hide. I want to have a good cry.

JOHAN   I'll go now if you like. We can meet tomorrow instead and go out and have dinner or something.

MARIANNE   Perhaps it would be better. No, stay after all. Besides, I don't have time tomorrow.

JOHAN *(Gently)*   Hey! I'm awfully fond of you.

MARIANNE *(Gently)*   Hey! I'm behaving like a child.

JOHAN *(Gently)*   It's all right again now. The situation is under control. We've pulled through the crisis.

MARIANNE   It's such a scrawl that I can hardly read my own writing. All this first part is nothing important . . . *(Reads aloud)* "Yesterday I was suddenly seized by an almost reckless gaiety and for the first time all this year I felt the old lust for life, the eagerness to know what the day would bring . . ." *(Skipping)* and so on and so on. *(Goes on reading)* "Suddenly I turned around and looked at the old picture of my school class, when I was ten. I seemed to be aware of something that had been lying in readiness for a long time but beyond my grasp. To my surprise I have to admit that *I don't know who I am.* I haven't the vaguest idea. I have always done what people told me. As far back as I can remember I've been obedient, adaptable, almost meek. Now that I think about it, I had one or two violent outbursts of self-assertion as a little girl. But I remember also that Mother punished all such lapses from convention with exemplary severity. For my sisters and me our entire upbringing was aimed at our being *agreeable.* I was rather ugly and clumsy and was constantly informed of the fact. By degrees I found that if I kept my thoughts to myself and was ingratiating and farsighted, such behavior brought its rewards. The really big deception, however, occurred during puberty. All my thoughts, feelings, and actions revolved round sex. I didn't let on about this to my parents, or to anyone at all for that matter. Then it became second nature to be deceitful, surreptitious, and secretive. My father wanted me to be a lawyer like himself. I once hinted that I'd prefer to be an actress. Or at any rate to have *something* to do with the theater. I remember they just laughed at me. So it has gone on and on. In my relations with other people. In my relations with men. The same perpetual dissimulation. The same desperate attempts to please everybody. I have never thought: What do *I* want? But always: What does *he* want me to want? It's not unselfishness as I used to think, but sheer cowardice, and what's worse—utter ignorance of

who I am. I have never lived a dramatic life, I have no gift
for that sort of thing. But for the first time I feel intensely
excited at the thought of finding out what exactly I want to
do with myself. In the snug little world where both Johan
and I have lived so unconsciously, taking everything for
granted, there is a cruelty and brutality implied which
frightens me more and more when I think back on it. Out-
ward security demands a high price: the acceptance of a
continuous destruction of the personality. (I think this ap-
plies especially to women; men have somewhat wider mar-
gins.) It is easy right at the outset to deform a little child's
cautious attempts at self-assertion. It was done in my case
with injections of a poison which is one hundred percent
effective: *bad conscience.* First toward Mother, then toward
those around me, and, last but not least, toward Jesus and
God. I see in a flash what kind of person I would have been
had I not allowed myself to be brainwashed. And I wonder
now whether I am hopelessly lost. Whether all the potential
for joy—joy for myself and others—that was innate in me
is dead or whether it's just asleep and can be awakened. I
wonder what kind of wife and woman I would have become
if I'd been able to use my resources as they were intended.
Would Johan and I have got married at all in that case? Yes,
I'm sure we would, because now that I think about it, we
were genuinely in love with each other in a devoted and
passionate way. Our mistake was that we didn't break out
of the family circle and escape far away and create something worthwhile on our own terms."
(MARIANNE *finishes reading and looks up from the notebook.* JOHAN
*is sitting with his head sunk on his chest and breathing deeply. He
is asleep. She gives a sad little smile and puts the notebook down
carefully. Then she finishes her brandy and, without waking him,
tiptoes out into the kitchen and starts putting the dishes in the
dishwasher. The phone rings. She hurries into the study and answers
in a whisper)*

MARIANNE   Hello. Oh, it's you. You weren't going to call this
evening. Are you jealous? You needn't be, I assure you. Do

I sound funny? No, I don't want to wake Johan. What? No, he's sitting. Sitting in the living room and sleeping like a little child. He is, really. My conversation bored him so much. No, don't come over, there's a dear. Don't be silly now, David. I'll see you tomorrow evening. Let's have dinner out and then go to a movie. It's been ages. Good. Will you call me up tomorrow morning as usual? If I sound a bit funny it's not really so strange. You can't expect me to stand here cooing into the phone. I don't know whether Johan has woken up. No, don't be idiotic, David. *(Laughs)* Precisely. I'll go in and wake my beau now and thank him for a nice evening, and then I'll pack him off home. You can call again in an hour. All right? Good. So long. What did you say? No, he hasn't even tried to kiss me, you needn't worry. It has been a very chaste evening. Bye!

(MARIANNE *goes back and wakes* JOHAN *gently. He is very ashamed and passes his hand time and again over his face)*

JOHAN   To think I damn well fell asleep. And what you were reading was so interesting too. Please forgive me, Marianne. Won't you read some more? I know you must be terribly hurt, but won't you read some more anyway?

MARIANNE   I think you ought to go home to bed now. *(With a smile)* I'm not a bit hurt. Really.

JOHAN   Yes, I'd better push off now.
(They stand rather at a loss and unhappy. He fiddles with his pipe. She has picked up a coffee cup)

MARIANNE   Perhaps you'll call up some time. If only for the children's sake.

JOHAN   Yes, sure. Yes, of course I will.

MARIANNE   It's always nice to see you, you know that.

JOHAN   If only Paula weren't so goddamn jealous. But still, she has reason. It's hard on her too.

MARIANNE   When will you know definitely about America?

JOHAN   In about a month.

MARIANNE   You can let me know what happens.

JOHAN   Yes, I'll phone you. Or write.

MARIANNE   And what are we going to do about the divorce? We must make up our minds.

JOHAN   *(Wearily)*   Are you going to marry again?

MARIANNE   *(Wearily)*   I don't know yet.

JOHAN   I'd rather wait before deciding. Don't you think so too?

MARIANNE   I don't know what I think. Sometimes I'm in despair. And then I think we ought to get divorced at once. And then sometimes I think rather hopefully that perhaps there's a chance we'll make it after all. *(At last they go out into the hall.* MARIANNE *is now very low.* JOHAN *embraces her; he too is in a state of utter confusion. Suddenly they start kissing each other.* MARIANNE *clings to him. They stagger against the wall. Smiles)* You'll stay the night. Won't you?

JOHAN   Yes, I'll stay the night.
(So they go to bed, and lie for a long time caressing each other with great tenderness and in silence. Then the phone rings in the study)

MARIANNE   Never mind the phone. It's nothing.

JOHAN   *(In a rather forced tone)*   Perhaps it's your lover. What can he want at this hour? Does he know I'm here?

MARIANNE   Of course he knows.

JOHAN   My God he's persistent.

MARIANNE   I'd better go and answer it after all. *(The telephone keeps on ringing.* MARIANNE *gets up quickly and puts on a dressing gown.* JOHAN *sees her go into the study—she leaves the door open—and hears what she is saying)* Hello. I can't talk now. Yes, Johan is still here. We've gone to bed, if you must know. So I imagine. What do you expect me to say? Yes, I'm sorry, it's true. I don't know. I'd be awfully glad if you didn't call up any more. I mean ever again. Try *for once* to behave like a grown-up man. Yes, it *is* a pity, I quite agree, but I really don't want to talk any more now. So long, David, take care of yourself.

(She flings down the phone and stands for a moment in thought, with her long red dressing gown and her hair loose, her right index finger against her cheek and illuminated by the table lamp. Then she gives a dry little laugh and puts the light out. She goes back to JOHAN *and sits on the edge of the bed. A smile)*

JOHAN   I couldn't help overhearing.

MARIANNE   You were meant to.

JOHAN   It was your lover, I gather.

MARIANNE   It was my *former* lover.

JOHAN   There was no need to say I was here.

MARIANNE   Perhaps you think I should have invited him. He was very anxious to come.

JOHAN   Are you in love with him?

MARIANNE   *(Gives him a long look)*   Sometimes you ask such goddamn silly questions that I could kill you on the spot.

JOHAN   Sorry, I'm sure.

MARIANNE   If you want to know all about my love life I'll gladly tell you.

JOHAN   Are you angry with me now?

MARIANNE   I'm not angry but I'm about to cry. The trouble with me is that I can't get angry. I wish that one day I could really lose my temper, as I sometimes feel I have every right to do. I think it would change my life. *(Pause)* But that's by the way. *(Sighs)* When you left me I had only one thought in my head: I wanted to die. I walked about that morning, it was just at dawn, and I thought: I'll never live through this. In a sudden mood of spite I wanted the children to die too. But then Karin woke up feeling peculiar and was sick and had a temperature. It was a blessing in disguise, let me tell you. Then she broke out in spots, it was the measles, and the best thing that could have happened. She was really quite ill, with a touch of pneumonia, so what with nursing her in the evenings and at night, and with my work at the office in the daytime, I was kept pretty busy and had no time left over to brood. Then I got a stomach ulcer and that was a good thing too, though I felt lousy. *(Pause)* Well, so the weeks passed. Then I met the doctor at a dinner party. I can't say I was particularly attracted, but he wouldn't leave me alone and talked to me about myself. So I was hooked. Since then I've been pretty unsettled, to be quite honest. There have been times when I've gone around in a state of almost insane erotic excitement. I even got myself a massage gadget and read pornography to try to ease the pressure, but it only made it worse. Nothing helped. Do you know why? I was so bound to you that every time I had someone else in bed I thought only of you. I'm not saying this to give you a bad conscience, but merely to tell you just how it was. Since you wanted me to be frank. I got tired of those men too, not only in bed. Sometimes I got a kick out of it while it lasted, especially if we'd been drinking. But I got tired of their talk too. You and I have always got along so well together when we've been talking or working or just sitting quietly. I got fed up with their talk, their bodies, their gestures and movements. To my mind they made fools of themselves and I felt sorry for them. *(Pause, reflection)* It was all pretty humiliating, to tell the truth. *(Pause again)* Well, then I met David and he was rather different. Also, he was younger than I and a bit childish. He was quite unlike the others, anyway. Moreover, he was inclined to be wild. I found it hard to defend myself, so I rather fell for him. He was an extraordinary mixture—kind and gentle and considerate and ruthless and violent, so I must admit he swept me off my feet. He was so nice to the children, too. We all got along awfully well together, and the girls liked him. It wasn't such a bad set-up and I began to forget you. *(Sits in silence, thinking)*

JOHAN   And it was good in bed, I gather?

MARIANNE   Not at first. He was so fierce that he scared me and everything went wrong. He made so many demands on me and wasn't in the least considerate or thoughtful or anything. Then suddenly I *liked* the way he didn't give a damn about me—though oddly enough he did in a strange intuitive way. I'm pretty sure he was unfaithful at times. Not that I cared. I never asked.

JOHAN   *(Gloomy)*   And now you've finished it off. What a pity!

MARIANNE   *(Gravely)*   I don't know that it is, really.

JOHAN   You'll probably make it up next week.

MARIANNE   I'm not so sure I want to. It's not him I want. You were talking about loneliness—about admitting that one is lonely. I don't believe in your gospel of loneliness. I think it's a sign of weakness.
(All this time she has been sitting at the foot of the bed with her back against the bed-end. Now she lifts both her hands and holds them in front of her face in a helpless gesture)

JOHAN   What is it? *(Pause)* What's wrong, Marianne?

MARIANNE   It's so humiliating . . .

JOHAN *(After a pause)*   What is?

MARIANNE   I don't know. *(Pulls herself together)* I'm thinking of the future, and then I think of you and me. I can't see how you're going to cope without me. Sometimes I feel quite desperate and think: *I must look after Johan.* He's my responsibility. It's up to me to see that Johan is all right. Only in that way will my life have a worthwhile meaning. One can't live alone and strong. One must have someone's hand to hold. Can't you *begin* to understand? I think we're making a mistake. I think we should work like hell to repair our marriage. As things are now we have a unique opportunity. We're wasting time. You're not to go away for three years without me. It would be too much for you. You're going to be so awfully afraid and uncertain if I don't look after you. I'm sorry to cry. I didn't mean to.
(JOHAN has sat up in bed and is caressing her knee clumsily. He sits bending forward with his head sunk, distressed and upset)

JOHAN   Sometimes I've puzzled over what can be wrong with me. I've wondered why I broke away from our marriage and why I fell in love with Paula and why I can't go back to you, now that it's over with Paula. But I can't arrive at an explanation. I'm completely in the dark. I'm fond of you, you know that, and sometimes I long for you most desperately. Yet it's as if there were a thick glass wall between us. I can see you, but I can't reach you. It's a sort of contempt—no, no, Marianne, I didn't mean that. You musn't take it literally. I express myself so badly. It's useless trying to explain. I only say the wrong things. I'll go now anyway.

MARIANNE   Can't you stay? We can lie side by side and hold hands. And we can talk about all sorts of unimportant little things. And by and by we'll fall asleep.

JOHAN *(Giving in)*   All right then. I'm terribly tired, as a matter of fact. I must just go to the bathroom. *(He gets up and shuffles out.* MARIANNE *smooths down the bed and opens the window a crack. Then she sets the alarm. She goes out into the kitchen and gets a bottle of mineral water and two glasses.* JOHAN *comes back)* I found some of my old pajamas in the cupboard. How nice to see them again.

MARIANNE   Good night, Johan. Sleep well.

JOHAN   Sleep well.

━━━━━

A few hours pass. Then MARIANNE *wakes up to find that* JOHAN *has switched on the bedside lamp and gotten up.*

MARIANNE   What is it? Can't you sleep?

JOHAN   No, not a hope, I'd better go home. I feel miserable lying here. I'm sorry. *(He has begun to dress.* MARIANNE *also gets out of bed. She opens the drawer of the bedside table and takes out a letter which she hands to him. He checks himself and looks at the envelope in astonishment)* Why, that's Paula's handwriting.

MARIANNE   It's a letter to me from Paula.

JOHAN   What nasty things has she been writing?

MARIANNE   Read the letter yourself. It came before she went to London. I wasn't going to show it to you, as she didn't want me to. But I feel I must after all. Read it. No, read it out loud—now.

JOHAN *(Reading aloud)*   "Dear Marianne—I suspect that you'll be surprised to get a letter from me and I want to say at the outset that I'm not writing with any ulterior motive. I took this assignment in London so that I could get away for a week and thereby break a vicious circle of jealousy and suspicion. I know that Johan will look you up the minute I've gone. I have only myself to blame, as I've consistently stopped him from seeing you and the children. If only one could rectify mistakes. But what is done cannot be undone. If one could only wipe out suffering that one has caused other people . . ." (JOHAN *stops reading. He hands the letter back to* MARIANNE *and gives a laugh*) Just like Paula. As smart as ever.

MARIANNE   I think she means what she's written. She says that she wants us to be friends. She says that she can't endure hostility and silence. And here at the end: "If Johan does wants to go back to his family now, I won't prevent him."

JOHAN   How touching. And most touching of all is that you believe her.

MARIANNE   Don't tell her I've shown you the letter! Please!

JOHAN   (*Taking the letter and reading*)   "Johan is the gentlest, kindest, and most affectionate person I have ever met. If there is such a thing as love, then I think I love him. Johan's difficulty is that deep down he is so unsure of himself. He is utterly lacking in self-confidence, although he tries to seem so capable and courageous and never complains." (*Finishes reading*) I've noticed that actually you can say anything you like about anyone at all. Somehow it always fits. Here, you can take the letter.
(*He finishes dressing in silence, goes out into the hall, and puts on his coat.* MARIANNE *remains sitting on the bed holding the letter.* JOHAN *comes back into the bedroom, stands in front of her, and lays his hand on her shoulder. She looks up at him. They don't know what to say. He strokes her cheek. She kisses his hand. Then he goes*)

FIFTH SCENE
The Illiterates

CHARACTERS

MARIANNE
JOHAN
NIGHT WATCHMAN

An extremely neutral room (regulation size). It is an evening in June. JOHAN *sits reading a report. He has a cold. There's a knock at the door. Before* JOHAN *has time to answer,* MARIANNE *storms in.*

MARIANNE   Sorry I'm late. But Daddy called just as I was leaving, and he went on and on and on. I said several times I was in a hurry, but he wouldn't listen. How are you?

JOHAN   I have a cold.

MARIANNE   Yes, you look pretty wretched.

JOHAN   At first I just had a sore throat that might have been anything and I thought, oh, it will go away. Then it turned into a runny nose and then went down into my chest. So now I cough all night long. I have a slight temperature and feel lousy. I very nearly phoned and put you off, but since you're going abroad I suppose it's essential to file the papers with the court before you leave, isn't it?

MARIANNE   Poor Johan. My heart bleeds for you. I hope Paula is looking after you properly.

JOHAN   She's also down with a cold. But with her it's a sort of gastric flu. It's all terribly romantic.

130

MARIANNE   You'll pull through, don't worry.

JOHAN   You seem in very good spirits.

MARIANNE   Hmm, I am, at that.

JOHAN   Any special reason?

MARIANNE   Oh, I'm always excited before a trip. And then it's spring. And I have a new coat and skirt. How do you like it, by the way? Smart, isn't it? Of course in this light you can't see the color properly, But do you like it?

JOHAN   Yes, it's very nice.

MARIANNE   I'm glad we could meet here in your workroom. It saves time, I mean.

JOHAN   It's not exactly cozy.

MARIANNE   Just the place for going through divorce papers. Now, if you'll just look at this. Here's the actual agreement that Henning has drawn up. It's word for word as we dictated it together.

JOHAN   Then I needn't read through it.

MARIANNE   One should always read before signing. Don't look so grumpy, Johan.

JOHAN   I'm not grumpy.

MARIANNE   You're as sulky as can be. Here's the inventory of goods and chattels we acquired jointly and how we've divided them up between us. It's only a reminder list. You needn't sign it.

JOHAN   It says here that you're to have Granny's wall clock. That's a mistake, anyway.

MARIANNE   My dear Johan, your grandmother gave it to me. We've discussed it, for that matter.

JOHAN   I can't recollect having discussed Granny's wall clock.

MARIANNE   If you're so attached to it, then keep it by all means. But it is actually mine.

JOHAN   No, for Christ's sake. You're right as always. Take the damned clock, I'm not going to squabble over trifles. *(Coughs)*

MARIANNE   Is there anything else you think I have wrongfully appropriated?

JOHAN *(Sulkily)*   Your sarcasm is wasted. I have a cold and I'm depressed. So there. Would you like a glass of fine old brandy?

MARIANNE   That's just what the doctor ordered.

JOHAN   Egerman gave me a bottle. He had been in Paris lecturing and was presented with a whole case by grateful colleagues. There we are. Skoal! Well, what do you say? God, I needed that!

MARIANNE   Mmm. I don't really care for brandy, but this is something special.

JOHAN   I feel better now.

MARIANNE *(After a pause)*   It's hard all the same.

JOHAN   What's hard?

MARIANNE   Getting divorced.

JOHAN   It's only a few goddamn papers.

MARIANNE   I still think it's hard. We've been living apart for ages. We've seen practically nothing of each other. We're agreed. Yet one has a bad conscience. Isn't it strange. Johan! Don't you think it's—

JOHAN *(Sadly)*   Yes, it's strange.

MARIANNE   On my way here I was in a good mood. I was determined not to cry. I wasn't going to let the situation get me down.

JOHAN   You said you had a bad conscience.

MARIANNE   Can't we sit over there on the sofa and put the overhead light out? The glare is frightful. How can you work in such a bleak room?

JOHAN   The sofa's not very comfortable either.

MARIANNE   Yes it is, if you put your feet up on a chair.

JOHAN   Is that comfy? Like some more brandy?

MARIANNE   Yes, please. Are you all alone here this evening? Is the whole place empty?

JOHAN   There's a night watchman.

MARIANNE   How nice.

JOHAN   What do you mean, nice?

MARIANNE   I don't know, just nice.

JOHAN   When you have a cold, nothing's nice.

MARIANNE   Oh, stop feeling sorry for yourself! You're not going to die of it. Skoal! This gets better and better.

JOHAN   You *are* in good spirits. I envy you.

MARIANNE   Yes, I think I am, though I'm not sure. *(Smiles)* To tell the truth, I'm rather in love.

JOHAN   Still that David?

MARIANNE   David? Oh, him! No, that's over and done with.

JOHAN   Oh.

MARIANNE   For another thing, I'm beginning to feel free of you. And that's a relief. A *great* relief.

JOHAN   What do you mean by that?

MARIANNE   Never mind. Give me a kiss.

JOHAN   I have a cold.

MARIANNE   Don't you remember that I never catch your germs? Give me a kiss. I want you to.

JOHAN *(Kissing her)*   Well, was it what you expected?

MARIANNE   Better. *(Unbuttoning her blouse)* Now put your hand on my breast. Like that. Nice?

JOHAN   Are you going to seduce me?

MARIANNE   That's exactly my plan. In this very place, at this very moment. On the carpet, wall-to-wall and everything. What do you say to that? Wouldn't that be nice? Why do you look so anxious? Scared of the night watchman? After all, we're still married. Come and lie on top of me. One should make love on the floor much more often. Can you lock the door? Come and lie down, my darling. There, isn't that a lovely feeling? *(Smiles)* My poor little husband, who leads such a miserable life. There, there, this is more like it, isn't it? Kiss me. I've always liked it when you kiss me. Now you lie on your back and I'll sit on top, then we'll come together. Shut your eyes. If you look at me I get so self-conscious. And hold your hands on my hips, like this. That's it. That feels lovely. Imagine if the night watchman came in! *(Smiles)* We'd ask him to join the party. We're so broadminded these days. And we have all night. Let's just drink and make love. And tomorrow we'll file the divorce papers.

(After they have made love they lie side by side facing each other. JOHAN *'s hand rests against her cheek.* MARIANNE *has closed her eyes but is still smiling)*

JOHAN   A penny for your thoughts.

MARIANNE   Mmm, I'm not telling.

JOHAN   Perhaps you're hungry?

MARIANNE   I always am.

JOHAN   What about a mixed grill and some beer? Doesn't that sound good?

MARIANNE   But you're not allowed to take me out to a restaurant.

JOHAN   I'm in Uppsala this evening with my students.

MARIANNE   In that case you may stand me to supper by all means. *(They are hilarious, tousled, and tipsy. They start putting their clothes and faces in order)*Is there a bathroom anywhere near?

JOHAN   Along the corridor to the left. You can't miss it.
  *(*MARIANNE *unlocks the door and disappears into the corridor.* JO-HAN *goes over to the desk and begins to fill his pipe. He lights it,*

glancing rather absentmindedly at the divorce papers which lie strewn over the desk. Suddenly the NIGHT WATCHMAN *is standing in the doorway)*

NIGHT WATCHMAN   Good evening, Professor.

JOHAN *(With a start)*   Heavens, it's you! Good evening.

NIGHT WATCHMAN   Working overtime, are we?

JOHAN   Er, yes.

NIGHT WATCHMAN   It's your secretary in the bathroom, I presume?

JOHAN   Eh? Oh yes, it's my secretary.

NIGHT WATCHMAN   Well, good night, Professor.

JOHAN   We're just going.

NIGHT WATCHMAN   You can stay all night, as far as I'm concerned.

JOHAN   We hadn't thought of doing so.

NIGHT WATCHMAN   Well, I wish you a nice Midsummer's Eve sir.

JOHAN   Same to you. Thank you. Good night.
(The NIGHT WATCHMAN *leaves.* JOHAN *sits down at the desk and begins to read the divorce agreement in earnest.* MARIANNE *comes in quietly and stands behind him, reading over his shoulder)*

MARIANNE   Let's sign the agreement and then go out and celebrate. Wouldn't that be a worthy end to a long and happy marriage?

JOHAN   I'd rather take the papers home and read through them quietly.

MARIANNE   What's this? Are we going to start chopping and changing after all our discussions?

JOHAN   You said yourself just now that one shouldn't sign anything without having read it through carefully. Didn't you?

MARIANNE   *(Irritated)*   All right, we'll sit down opposite each other and read through the whole thing from A to Z. So that you can see I haven't cheated you in some mysterious fashion. *(Sits down crossly)*

JOHAN   Why are you so cross?

MARIANNE   I'm not in the least cross. Well, let's start.

JOHAN   You are. You're in a filthy temper.

MARIANNE   All right, I'm in a filthy temper, but I shall try to control it, since I'm used to controlling myself toward you and your whims. *(Blandly)* Can we leave this boring discussion now and get on with the reading. It's rather late, at that, and I have a busy day tomorrow.

JOHAN   So now we're not going to have supper?

MARIANNE   No, thank you. I'd rather not. I'm so grateful for the favors already bestowed upon me.

JOHAN   Whose whims now?

MARIANNE   Look here, Johan. *(Controlling herself)* No, don't speak. There's no point. I'll try to keep my temper. *(Sweetly)* Now, we'll put the papers in this envelope, like this, and you take them home with you and then you and Paula can go through the wording carefully together and see that I haven't diddled you.

JOHAN   Why, Marianne, what the hell's the matter?

MARIANNE   Nothing.

JOHAN   We were such good friends a moment ago.

MARIANNE   *(Holding a tight rein on herself)*   Exactly. By the way, don't forget it's Eva's birthday on Tuesday.

JOHAN   Am I in the habit of forgetting the children's birthdays?

MARIANNE   No, it has never happened, as I have always re-
minded you in good time. I'd be grateful if you'd kindly pay
for her trip to France this summer. I can't afford it.

JOHAN   How much will it cost?

MARIANNE   I think about two thousand kronor.

JOHAN   What! Are you out of your mind? Where am I going
to get two thousand kronor suddenly? It's out of the question.

MARIANNE   Then you can ask your mother.

JOHAN   I've already borrowed far too much from her.

MARIANNE   Well, I have no money anyway. It cost me over a
thousand kronor to have Karin's teeth fixed.

JOHAN   Can't they get their teeth seen to at school?

MARIANNE   You know as well as I do why Karin refuses to go
to the school dentist.

JOHAN   Eva will just have to cancel her trip. *I* don't have any
money. It won't hurt her to learn that you can't have everything you point to in this world. She's so goddamn spoiled
for that matter that it's not true. *And* ill-mannered. She went
to see Mother last week and Mother phoned me afterwards
and was quite shattered at the kid's behavior.

MARIANNE   *(Capitulating)*   Oh, did she say that? Yes, it's hopeless. But she's at a difficult age.

JOHAN   I do think you might teach the girls a few manners.
But you let them boss you around just as they like.

MARIANNE   It's not so easy, let me tell you. They say I'm never at home to look after them. But I do try to be with them as much as I can. They're always angry with me. It's as if everything were my fault.

JOHAN   You should make them respect you. Anyway, they don't thank you for letting them do just as they like.

MARIANNE   Oh, don't talk nonsense. Isn't it better that I have their confidence? We do talk about everything. And for that I'm grateful. Why worry about trifles like manners and discipline and what you call being spoiled.

JOHAN   Anyhow, I'm not going to pay for Eva's trip to France. You can tell her that.

MARIANNE   Tell her yourself.

JOHAN   Why? You have the custody of the children. I have to fork out a hell of a big maintenance, which incidentally I have to pay taxes on and which is completely ruining me. So I don't see why I should have a lot of idiotic expenses on top of that. There's nothing to that effect in the divorce agreement, at any rate. Or is there?

MARIANNE   It's not the children's fault if we're worse off because you went off with another woman.

JOHAN   I never expected that remark from you.

MARIANNE   No, I'm sorry. It was crude of me.

JOHAN   Forget it. I will speak to our daughter. The difficulty is that we have no means of communication. Whenever she visits me she lolls on the sofa and reads *Donald Duck*. Or sprawls in an easy chair and watches TV. If I try to talk to her she mumbles something in a monosyllable as if she were a half-wit. Paula can't get any answer out of her at all. I think the girl is detestable, to be blunt. The only thing that makes her condescend to answer in a sentence with subject, predicate, and direct object is if I bribe her with money or treat her to the movies. Otherwise she chatters away on the phone to her friends for hours. At any rate I have no paternal feelings. Though I must admit she has grown pretty. No, it's much easier with Karin. Though she's so damned childish. Do you think perhaps she's a bit retarded? I'm beginning to be worried.

MARIANNE How stupid you sound when you talk about the children like that. Stupid and childish.

JOHAN Well, I am *not* amused. I brought them into the world by mistake and since then I've paid a small fortune for their upkeep. That must suffice. I refuse to play the fond father and I permit myself to dislike the children as much as they dislike me. Who has said that *I* must always be the one to take the first step toward contact and affection and love and all that? No, I prefer to act my part of wallet on two legs. At least that doesn't give me a bad conscience, seeing that I'm practically bankrupt with all I have to cough up. And that's as it should be. If you make a blunder, you have to pay. And if, as in this case, you make two blunders, then it costs you double. I don't mind telling you that I loathe my stupid, spoiled, brainless, lazy, and selfish daughters. Anyway, the feeling is reciprocated. *(Pause)* Why don't you say something? Are you angry now?

MARIANNE I'm thinking back.

JOHAN Thinking back?

MARIANNE It used to be different. *(Quickly)* I mean as regards the children. Do you remember? How pleased you were when I plodded around with my big belly. And how eager you were for Eva to have a baby sister or brother. Do you remember all you used to do for the girls when they were little? Do you remember how you helped me look after

them? You and I did everything between us and as a result
the nanny that Mother had hired gave notice in sheer des-
peration. You spent all your time with the children, you
played with them, read them fairy tales, you were so gentle
and kind and patient. Much more patient than I was. Do
you remember how worried you were over every little ill-
ness? You had a much better way with them than I did. And
they loved you. Do you remember our Saturday evenings
together? *(Sadly)* Why did things turn out like this? What
went wrong? When did the children get bored with you?
When did you get bored with them? What became of all the
love and solicitude? And all the joy? Think of that summer
when we gadded about the Mediterranean in your old rattle-
trap of a car and had the two small girls with us. And
camped out. Remember those August nights on the coast of
Spain, when we slept in the open, all four of us close together? Remember how nice and warm it was and what fun
we had?

JOHAN   There's no use crying over spilt milk. Children grow
up, relations are broken off. Love gives out, the same as
affection, friendship, and solidarity. It's nothing unusual. It
just is so.

MARIANNE   Sometimes I feel that you and I were both born
with silver spoons in our mouths, but we've squandered our
resources and suddenly find ourselves poor and bitter and
angry. We must have gone wrong somewhere, and there was
no one to tell us what we did.

JOHAN   I'll tell you something banal. We're emotional illiter-
ates. And not only you and I—practically everybody, that's
the depressing thing. We're taught everything about the
body and about agriculture in Madagascar and about the
square root of pi, or whatever the hell it's called, but not a
word about the soul. We're abysmally ignorant, about both
ourselves and others. There's a lot of loose talk nowadays to
the effect that children should be brought up to know all

about brotherhood and understanding and coexistence and equality and everything else that's all the rage just now. But it doesn't dawn on anyone that we must first learn something about ourselves and our own feelings. Our own fear and loneliness and anger. We're left without a chance, ignorant and remorseful among the ruins of our ambitions. To make a child aware of its soul is something almost indecent. You're regarded as a dirty old man. How can you ever understand other people if you don't know anything about yourself? Now you're yawning, so that's the end of the lecture. I had nothing more to say anyway. Some more brandy? Then we'll decide what to do about that supper.

MARIANNE   Yes, please. Incidentally I don't agree with you, but never mind. I don't believe in all that talk about awareness. What's the point of making people more nervous than they are already? You say that knowledge is security. Nonsense. Knowledge gives a wider choice and more anguish.

JOHAN   *(Coughing)*   Damn this cough. Oh, before I forget. I have something funny to tell you. That guest professorship has gone to hell. Not that it matters. But still.

MARIANNE   Why, Johan, what a terrible shame!

JOHAN   *(Drinking)*   Oh, I don't know. I was pretty disappointed, naturally. As usual there has been some goddamn hanky-panky. First the trip was postponed, and that was nothing to make a fuss about. Then suddenly there was no money. Then next thing I knew they'd sent Akerman! And fuck me. *(Laughs)* Just goes to show. Skoal!

MARIANNE   Poor old Johan. When did that happen?

JOHAN   In May. I had to request a new leave of absence, and it was difficult. Then Öhberg suggested that I apply directly to the chancellor of the university. Well, eventually they told me that Akerman was going instead. Granted, he has done a bit more research recently. But obviously there's some funny business somewhere. It smells a mile away.

MARIANNE   Poor Johan, I *am* sorry.

JOHAN *(Beginning to harp)*   I don't understand the mentality. A couple of weeks ago we were supposed to go to a convention in Oslo. Suddenly the department butts in and tells us we can't go. A, we're not getting any money, and B, we're to stay at home and get on with our job. *(Sips his brandy)* That's no way to talk to us, for Christ's sake! We're not a lot of lazy school kids playing hooky. I went up to the department to have the matter out. I've never known anything like it. I asked to see the minister of education but he didn't have time, so I had to content myself with some confounded underlings. You should have seen them! You should have seen the way they behaved. At least I was taught manners. And I'm a good bit older. There they sat in their shirt-sleeves, smoking and looking bored and supercilious. And their language! That undersecretary is a complete nitwit. They practically laughed me down. In the end I didn't know what I was saying, so I walked out. That's how they treat you nowadays. You're just a cipher. *(Drinks)* People like me have become inconvenient. And of course we're not of the right political shade. Not progressive. Not to the left of left. Overage. Out of the race. I could die laughing. *(Drinks)* I'll be forty-five this summer. I can reasonably expect to live for another thirty years. But viewed objectively I'm already a corpse. For the next twenty years I'll go around embittering my own life and other people's merely by existing. I am regarded as an expensive, unproductive unit which by rights should be got rid of by rationalization. And this is supposed to be the prime of life, when you could really make yourself useful, when you've gained a little experience. Shit, no. Throw the bugger out. Or let him creep around until he rots. I'm so goddamn tired, Marianne. If I had the guts I'd make a clean break and move to the country or ask for a job as teacher in a small town. Sometimes I wish I could . . .

(Drinks) Well, that's my sad story. *(Laughs)* Paula has a very ambivalent attitude toward the situation. And sometimes she says I'm a shit and starts packing her things. I don't know which of the alternatives would give me most relief. Anyway, I think she has a lover. Not that I care. I'm not jealous any more. I'm not really anything any more. I hardly know who I am now. Someone spat on me and I drowned in the spittle. *(Laughs)*

MARIANNE   It's an extraordinary thing . . .

JOHAN   What's extraordinary?

MARIANNE   Here I sit listening to you. And by rights I should feel something. But I don't feel anything. Faint sympathy, at most. On my way here this evening I suddenly got the idea of sleeping with you to see if I felt anything. And all I felt was good-natured friendship. Do you know what I think, Johan? I'm in the process of becoming free from you. It has taken a long time and been horribly painful. But I think I'm free now and can begin to live my own life. And how glad I am!

JOHAN   Allow me to congratulate you.

MARIANNE   I don't know why I'm saying this. And I suppose it's pretty callous of me to say it now, just when you've told me that you're going through a bad stretch. But oddly enough I don't care. I've considered you far too much during our married life. I think consideration killed off love. Has it struck you that we never quarreled? I think we even thought it was vulgar to quarrel. No, we sat down and talked so sensibly to each other. And you, having studied more and knowing more about the mind, told me what I *really* thought. What I felt *deep down.* I never understood what you were talking about. I merely felt a heavy weight like a sorrow. Had I allowed myself not to react with a bad conscience, I'd have known that everything we said and did to each other was wrong. Do you remember after Karin was born? When we suddenly couldn't make love any more? We sat down so prudently and explained so prudently to each other that it was quite natural. That it was only to be expected after two pregnancies one on top of the other. And all our subsequent discussions as to why we didn't get any pleasure out of making love. Neither of us realized that they were warnings. Red lights and stop signals were flashing all around us. But we only thought that was as it should be. We declared ourselves satisfied.

JOHAN   I think that these retrospective expositions are awfully boring and unnecessary.

MARIANNE *(Shouting)*   Your idiotic sarcasms nearly drive me mad. Must you always be the one to decide what is suitable or convenient? It serves you right if things have gone wrong. I'm *glad* Paula has a lover. You can commit suicide for all I care, though I expect you're too much of a coward. Well, well, so there you sit with tears in your eyes. And it leaves me cold! You can be made to feel what it's like for once. Feel what I've gone through.

JOHAN *(Calmly)*   Jesus, how I hate you really. I remember thinking it quite often: Jesus, how I hate her. Especially when we had made love and I had felt your indifference and knew you'd been thinking of something else. And we'd be out in the bathroom, with you sitting there naked on the bidet washing and washing away that nasty stuff you had got from me which you said smelled so awful. Then I would think: I hate her, her body, her movements. I could have struck you. I was itching to smash that white, hard resistance that radiated from you. But we chatted away so amicably to each other, joking about the nice times we had together in spite of everything.

MARIANNE   Then perhaps you can explain to me why I now have a man. And I love him. I love his body, I like his smells.

I do everything he asks me to. I long for him to take hold of me, for him to touch my breasts. Do you remember I only allowed you to touch my breasts in a special way, I shuddered when you fondled me unexpectedly, when you did anything that hadn't been agreed on. It's not so any more.

JOHAN   Just you wait and see. After a time you will marry him and before you know where you are you'll start in the same way with him. You wait and see. It's deep-rooted, that is. You'll start looking around for a new lover who can once again free you from that loathing.

MARIANNE   I know you're wrong. And I know that we could have come through those difficulties. They were not confined to our sex life. They were symptoms of other tensions. And those we'd have tried to clear up together. But we were so hopelessly considerate, we failed before we'd even started.

JOHAN *(Angry)*   There's such a thing as ordinary simple affection. There's such a thing as normal, natural sensuality, physical desire. But you don't know that. For you it's all blocked, shut off.

MARIANNE   I agree it has been so with you, but can *I* help that? Do you imagine I wasn't just as miserable about it as you were? I used to think: Must it be like this for us? Must it be so wretched? Then we'd console ourselves with the thought that after all sex was only of secondary importance, and that we got along well together in every other way. What self-deception, Johan. Nothing could be right when we could no longer make love.

JOHAN   You're forgetting certain things which it may be unpleasant to mention in this connection.

MARIANNE   Then perhaps you would kindly enlighten me.

JOHAN   Do you know what you did all along? *You exploited your sex organs.* They became a commodity. If you let me make love to you one day, the implication was that you'd be spared the next day. If I had been nice and helpful, I was rewarded with a lay. If I had been disagreeable or dared to criticize in any way, you got your own back by closing shop. What I put up with! It's grotesque when I think of the way you carried on. Christ! You were worse than any whore.

MARIANNE   But you wouldn't face the truth.

JOHAN   What goddamn truth, may I ask? Is it some sort of female truth? A truth with patent pending?

MARIANNE *(Furious)*   You're crazy. I really think you're out of your mind. Do you imagine that you can go on wiping your feet on me indefinitely? Am I always to be a substitute for your mother? All that goddamn harping on how I neglected our home and put my job first.

JOHAN   That's not true!

MARIANNE   During the first years of our marriage it was nothing but nag, nag, nag, both from you and your parents and from my own mother. All you succeeded in doing was to give me a bad conscience. I had a bad conscience at work and a bad conscience at home. Then I was expected to have a bad conscience because I didn't make love properly either. I was hedged in on all sides. Nothing but grumbling and nagging and demanding and—*Oh!* you son of a bitch! And if I got my own back with my sex organs, as you say, was it so strange? I was fighting against hopeless odds all the time: you and my mother and your parents and the whole of this goddamn society. I could never do what I wanted. There was always something in the way. When I think of what I endured and what I've at last broken free from, I could scream. And I tell you this: *Never again, never again, never again, never again.* You sit there whining about intrigues and having been double-crossed. It serves you right, it serves you damn well right. And I hope you have it rammed down your throat that you're a useless parasite.

JOHAN You're being utterly grotesque.

MARIANNE So what? That's how I've become. But the difference between my grotesqueness and yours is that I don't give in. I intend to keep on, you see. I intend to live in reality just as it is. For if there's one thing I like more than anything else on earth, it's to *live*. I enjoy overcoming difficulties and setbacks. And I don't ask for consideration. I don't give a damn for fine words and diplomacy.

JOHAN *(Snatching up the divorce agreement)* I'm glad we don't need to feel sympathy any longer. Glad we can throw all our bad conscience on the garbage pile. We're getting quite human. The whole trouble was that you and I ever met in the first place. That we fell in love and decided to live together. What a glorious fiasco right from the start. So the sooner we sign this paper the better, then we have only to divide up the silver and old wedding presents and say good-bye, and a pity it was all such a ghastly mistake from beginning to end.

MARIANNE I'm not responsible for you. I live my own life and I'm capable of looking after myself and the children. Do you suppose I don't grasp what you've been sitting here saying all evening: *You don't want a divorce!*

JOHAN *(Caught)* I never heard anything so absurd!

MARIANNE If it's so absurd then you can prove the opposite by signing the papers here and now.

JOHAN All right.

MARIANNE Johan! Be honest now! Look at me! Look at me,

Johan. You've changed your mind? You don't want us to divorce, do you? You thought we might pick up our marriage again. You were going to suggest something of the kind this evening. Go on, admit it.

JOHAN   Well, suppose I did have thoughts in that direction. Is it a crime? I confess I'm beaten. Is *that* what you want to hear? I'm tired of Paula. I'm homesick. Oh, I know, Marianne. You needn't put on that smile. I'm a failure and I'm going downhill and I'm scared and homeless. This isn't the right moment to ask you to go on with the marriage. I know what you're going to say. But you asked me. And I'm giving you a straight answer. I was bound to you in a different and deeper way than I realized. I was dependent on all those things that are called home and family and regular life and quiet everyday routine. I'm tired of living alone.

MARIANNE   Alone?

JOHAN   Loneliness with Paula is worse than real loneliness. I can't endure either of them. I can't talk about this. You know it all anyway. *(Silence)*

MARIANNE   *(After a pause)*   I wonder how it would turn out.

JOHAN   I know that it would turn out much better than it has ever been. I know that we would be much more concerned about each other. Don't you think so? *(Pause)* Don't you think so?

MARIANNE   After a week or two we'd slip back into the old groove, our old nagging, our old aggressions. All our good resolutions would be forgotten. We wouldn't have learned anything. Everything would be the same as before. Or worse. It would be a mistake.

JOHAN   How can you be so sure?

MARIANNE How many times must I repeat that I don't feel anything for you, other than rudimentary sympathy. *(Indignant)* I don't want you to entreat me. I'm not certain that ... I'm not certain that I could cope. And that would be the worst thing that could happen.

JOHAN Well, let's try.

MARIANNE *(Angry)* Do you remember when I begged and implored you to come back? Do you remember how I groveled and wept and pleaded? I even turned religious for a time and prayed to God to let me have you back. Do you remember our meetings and your pretexts and half-truths, which merely showed your complete indifference all the more clearly.

JOHAN I didn't know any better then. You can't reproach me for that now.

MARIANNE *(Angry)* Reproach! What a fantastic word, Johan. Do you know what I think? I think you are feeble-minded and naïve. Do you suppose that I've gone through all I have and come out on the other side and started a life of my own which every day I'm thankful for, just to take charge of you and see that you don't go to the dogs because you're so weak and full of self-pity? If I didn't think you were so deplorable I'd laugh at you. When I think of what you've done to me during the last few years, I feel sick with fury. Go on, look at me. I'm proof against that gaze of yours. I've hardened myself. If you knew how many times I've dreamt I battered you to death, that I murdered you, that I stabbed you, that I kicked you. If you only knew what a goddamn relief it is to say all this to you at last.

JOHAN *(Smiling suddenly)* You know, you're awfully pretty when you're angry like that.

MARIANNE That's nice to know. *(More graciously)* Though *you* just look comical. What's more, you have lipstick on your cheek.

JOHAN   If I understand correctly, you'd prefer to see the divorce go through.

MARIANNE *(On the verge of laughing)*   That's *exactly* how I'd like to sum up what I've already said.

JOHAN   Some more brandy?

MARIANNE   Heavens, we've nearly emptied the bottle! It's not surprising that I feel emancipated and a little peculiar. How do *you* feel?

JOHAN   Oh, not so bad. I think my cold has gone. At any rate, I haven't coughed for some time.

MARIANNE *(Drinking)*   Well, to talk sensibly . . .

JOHAN   So what you said earlier wasn't sensible?

MARIANNE   It wasn't sensible, but it was true and necessary, as you must see.

JOHAN   I'm sitting here seeing as hard as I can.

MARIANNE   To talk sensibly, then. To say something reasonable, you should be glad I've made myself free and that I want to live my own life. I think you should do exactly the same. You should free yourself from the past, every bit of it. And start fresh under completely different conditions. *At this very moment* you have a marvelous chance.

JOHAN   Will you answer me something?

MARIANNE   Now you're sounding all pathetic again.

JOHAN   What's the use? I mean, to start fresh, as you say. I have no desire to.

MARIANNE *(Hesitating)*   What do you mean now?

JOHAN   Only what I've already said three or four times this evening, though you haven't bothered to listen. I have no desire to start fresh, I have no curiosity about what's ahead of me.

MARIANNE *(Beaten)*   You're only saying that because you're depressed and have had setbacks. You just want sympathy.

JOHAN *(With a smile)*   You've hit the nail on the head.

MARIANNE   When I think of the person I was only a few years ago, it's like someone altogether different. When you and I made love this evening I felt as if I were doing it with a stranger. Funny, isn't it? To be honest, it was rather exciting. Perhaps one day we'll be very good friends. And we'll gradually learn to know each other as the people we *really* are and not that horrible . . .

JOHAN   Horrible what?

MARIANNE   I mean that masked thing.

JOHAN   Masked thing?

MARIANNE   If only we could meet as the people we were meant to be. And not as people who try to play the parts that all sorts of powers have assigned us.

JOHAN   I'm afraid it's impossible. The masking starts in the cradle and goes on all through life. No one in the world can find himself, as you say.

MARIANNE   It's not true. I live a much more honest life now
than I've ever done.

JOHAN   And happier?

MARIANNE   All that talk about happiness is nonsense. My
greatest happiness is to eat a good dinner.

JOHAN *(Shaking his head)*   I'm not like you.

MARIANNE *(Suddenly, after a long pause)*   Don't you see that the
whole of this situation frightens me? I feel horribly tempted
to put out my hand and tear up that divorce agreement.
Time and again I think: Why do *I* think I have the right to
maintain a selfish life of my own? Do I really *imagine* I have

a mission outside you and the children? Wouldn't it be tempting to start all over again together? I'm much stronger now and more independent. I could really be of help to you when you're having a rough time of it. *(Her hands in front of her face)* I feel such tenderness for you, Johan. *(Desperately)* I must be out of my mind. I know that we must get a divorce. Wisdom and common sense tell me that we must. *(Taking his hands)* It's intolerable.

JOHAN *(Humbly)*   I think I understand.

MARIANNE *(Shaking her head)*   Let's not talk about it.

JOHAN   No.

MARIANNE   Well, what shall we do about that supper?

JOHAN   I'm too drunk to go anywhere. Can't we sit here together for a while longer?

MARIANNE   Why not. As long as you don't make me sentimental.

JOHAN   Can't we go home?

MARIANNE   You mean home to my place?

JOHAN   Of course I mean home to your place.

MARIANNE *(Shaking her head)*   No.

JOHAN *(Drunk)*   Why not?

MARIANNE   Because I have a man who is sitting waiting for me, and he's going to be pretty upset that I reek of brandy and that I'm so late and that the papers aren't signed.

JOHAN   Is he jealous?

MARIANNE   Not particularly. *(Smiles)* But he knows my maso-
chistic nature. Do you know what he said before I left? He
kissed me and said: "You and your husband will make love.
And you'll come home with a guilty conscience and you
won't have signed the papers. And you'll give me up."

JOHAN   Are you going to tell him we've made love together?

MARIANNE   No. *(Smiles)* No, I don't think I will.

JOHAN   God, I'm tired.

MARIANNE *(Matter-of-factly)*   We've had too much to drink. If
we were sensible we'd go for a brisk walk in the fresh air
before going home to our respective soulmates.

JOHAN   You really are fantastic.

MARIANNE   No, I just have an incurable passion for what's
healthy. Come along, my dear. Let's go.

JOHAN   And the papers?

MARIANNE   When I came here I was determined to have our
divorce put through at all costs. In some way I've changed
my mind.

JOHAN   That's generous of you.

MARIANNE   Not in the way you think.

JOHAN   In what way then?

MARIANNE   I think I had an idea of remarrying. I'm not sure,
but I think so. My friend who's at home waiting for me now
suits me in every way. We get along well together and the
girls like him. He himself has been divorced for many years
and not long ago he suggested that he and I should get

married. I must say I was tempted. *(Pause)* It's so silly with these papers. They mean nothing at all really. Take them, Johan. Tear them up if you like. It's all the same to me whether I bear your name or my own or someone else's.

JOHAN   God, what a sermon!

MARIANNE   You're right. Shall we go?

JOHAN   I don't mind signing the papers.

MARIANNE   Do as you like. I don't care.

JOHAN   Don't go!

MARIANNE   It's late. Can I call a cab?

JOHAN   You must dial zero first, then you'll get an outside line.

MARIANNE   *(Phoning)* Good evening. Will you send a cab to Malmrosgatan forty-five, please? It's coming at once? Thank you. *(Puts down the receiver)* Can I give you a ride? You'd better not take your own car. You've had too much to drink.

JOHAN   I'll stay for a while.

MARIANNE   No, don't, Johan. Come with me now. It's not good for you to sit here alone brooding.

JOHAN   Never mind what I do.

MARIANNE   Come along, Johan.

JOHAN   Why don't you stay a while longer?

MARIANNE   I don't want to stay any longer.

JOHAN   Please don't go.

MARIANNE   Please don't start that, Johan. You're just tired and drunk.

JOHAN   Don't go, please.

MARIANNE   Let me past!

JOHAN   I'm not letting you go.

MARIANNE   Don't be a fool!

JOHAN   Don't be a fool yourself.

MARIANNE   Even in our marriage we never behaved in this stupid way, Johan. Don't let's start now. Please give me the key.

JOHAN   I don't give a damn what you say. Now I can see Marianne's well-ordered brain clicking away! What do I do now? Has he gone mad? Is he going to hit me?

MARIANNE   If you really want to know, all I think is that you're screamingly funny.

JOHAN   Oh, funny am I? Then why don't you laugh? I think you look scared if anything.

MARIANNE   At least let me call and cancel the cab.

JOHAN   Why? It will wait for ten minutes and then drive off. Sit down and take it easy. This is going to take a long time, I promise you.

MARIANNE   All right, I don't mind. Well, what do you want to say now?

JOHAN   Nothing. I just want to look at you.

MARIANNE   Go ahead. *(With a mocking smile)* As a matter of fact, it's just what I might have expected from someone like you. I wonder how many times in my profession I've warned wives seeking a divorce against being alone with their wronged husbands. I must confess I never thought I'd land in that situation myself.

JOHAN   Shut up!

MARIANNE   Do you think I'm afraid? *(Shakes her head)* If you want to know, I couldn't care less about what you're going to do.

JOHAN   Shut up, I said! *(He strikes her)*

MARIANNE   You crazy fool! *(She strikes back. A fight breaks out. A brutal, reckless, vicious brawl, which goes on and on until they are both exhausted. They are in a violent fury, but played out and covered in blood. They have sunk down panting in different corners of the room)* You must give me the key so that I can go to the bathroom and try and stanch the blood.

JOHAN   I'm not letting you out.

MARIANNE   Give me the key, you big fucking slob. You goddamn shit.
(He knocks her down on to the floor and kicks her savagely. She tries to shield her face with her hands)

JOHAN   I could kill you. *(Shouts)* I could kill you! I could kill you! *(Then he tires. She is lying motionless, huddled up. Suddenly it is very quiet in the white, bare room. The light glares from the ceiling. Overturned furniture. Blood-stains on the carpet. The objects from the desk strewn everywhere. Silence)* Are you all right?

MARIANNE   It was my own fault. Will you please let me out now?
(JOHAN unlocks the door and she goes out into the dark corridor. He

sits down, his hands trembling violently. Again and again he takes very deep breaths, as though he were suffocating in rarefied air)

JOHAN *(Calling)*   Shall I help you?

MARIANNE *(From outside)*   No, please don't come here. *(He gets up slowly and goes over to the desk. Hunts about for a while. Finds the divorce papers and signs his name on the original and copies.* MARIANNE *comes in, having patched herself up as well as she could. She signs her name beside his. Then she folds the papers and puts them into her briefcase, which she clips shut. She puts on her gloves)* I'll see that the papers are filed in court as soon as possible.

JOHAN   Thank you, I'd appreciate that.

MARIANNE   Well, so long.

JOHAN   So long.

MARIANNE *(Turning in the doorway)*   We should have started fighting long ago. It would have been much better.

SIXTH SCENE

In the Middle of the Night in a Dark House Somewhere in the World

CHARACTERS

MARIANNE
JOHAN
EVA
ARNE
MARIANNE'S MOTHER

A few years later. MARIANNE *is paying a visit to her mother.*

MARIANNE Hello, Mummy dear.

MOTHER Hello.

MARIANNE How's your foot?

MOTHER Oh, the pain has gone. But naturally I feel handicapped.

MARIANNE When did the doctor think you could start work again?

MOTHER Not until next week.

MARIANNE Then you must arm yourself with patience.

MOTHER I just sit here and get nowhere.

MARIANNE Can you get any sleep at night?

MOTHER Well, the foot makes it difficult for me to turn in bed. But I mustn't complain. Would you like some tea? Miss Alm got the tray ready half an hour ago. So I've already had mine.

MARIANNE My dear, I'm awfully sorry to be so late, but I had a client I couldn't get rid of. And occasionally one must make time to listen.

MOTHER   Why, of course. I quite understand.

MARIANNE   The tea is still hot.

MOTHER   Shall I make you some toast?

MARIANNE   No thanks.

MOTHER   A piece of cake then?

MARIANNE   No thanks. I'm dieting.

MOTHER   How ridiculous.

MARIANNE   And I do exercises for half an hour every morning. And Henrik and I play tennis twice a week. It's very good for me.

MOTHER   Oh, there's something I must ask you since you're here. Are you coming to the interment of the ashes?

MARIANNE   When will it be?

MOTHER   We thought the eighteenth.

MARIANNE   Let me see now ... *(Refers to her pocket diary)* Hmm, that's difficult. I have a court case that morning and it's bound to drag on. Is Daddy to be buried at Uppsala?

MOTHER   That was his wish. Your brothers and sisters are coming.

MARIANNE   But Mummy dear, the interment is merely a formality. You can't expect me to play hooky from work just because of that.

MOTHER   It depends how you look at it.

MARIANNE   Can't we change the day then?

MOTHER   All the others could come. And as you know, April eighteenth was your father's and my anniversary. We were married on April eighteenth thirty-nine years ago. Perhaps you had forgotten?

MARIANNE   Won't it all be needlessly upsetting?

MOTHER   Not for me.

MARIANNE   In any case, I can't come.

MOTHER   Well then, that's that.

MARIANNE   Karin and Eva send their love. They promised to look in after school tomorrow.

MOTHER *(Brightens)*   Oh, how nice. Just imagine—Eva called to see me the day before yesterday with her boyfriend. She was actually wearing a dress and was quite the young lady. Her friend seems nice too. They stayed talking for a whole hour. I find it harder with Karin. But then she's the image of her grandfather.

MARIANNE   Poor Daddy.

MOTHER   I didn't mean to say anything disparaging about your father. Especially now that he is dead.

MARIANNE   I didn't think you did.

MOTHER   I've thought quite a lot about our marriage. Particularly sitting here with my foot, when I've had time to reflect.

MARIANNE   And what conclusion have you reached?

MOTHER   None at all, really. And that's what surprises me.

MARIANNE   What do you mean?

MOTHER   We had a good life. Sometimes we fell out, it's true, but we never quarreled. We never stooped to humiliating and insulting each other. We kept silent instead. And it was best like that. By degrees the hostility faded away and we forgot our differences. Neither Fredrik nor I was one to nurse a grievance.
(Pause)

MARIANNE   No.

MOTHER   Of course I miss him. But actually I don't feel any more alone now than when he was alive.

MARIANNE   I'm sorry to hear that.

MOTHER   Why? Both of us were kept busy. He with his affairs, I with mine.

MARIANNE   May I ask you something, Mummy?

MOTHER   Ask me anything you like.

MARIANNE   But please don't think I'm being tactless.

MOTHER   I won't think that.

MARIANNE   How was it in bed, for you and Daddy?

MOTHER *(Pause)*   He was more interested than I was.

MARIANNE   Well?

MOTHER *(Irritated)*   What more do you want to know? He took what he wanted. And I let him have his way. I never refused him. I considered it my duty to be at his disposal. Anyway, he had other women. At times it was rather horrible.

MARIANNE   And you?

MOTHER   I?

MARIANNE   Did you have other men?

MOTHER   After Fredrik and I were engaged I fell in love with another man and wanted to break it off. But Mother and Father didn't want me to do anything rash. So that was that.

MARIANNE   Haven't you ever hated Daddy?

MOTHER   Hated him? What do you mean?

MARIANNE   When you got married, you both signed a contract entirely in his favor. Haven't you ever hated him for that transaction?

MOTHER   I liked him. Besides, we were as blind as kittens. Neither of us realized what we were embarking on.

MARIANNE   But Mummy, it's not possible!

MOTHER   He had his faults. So did I. *(Pause)* No, it's not that.

MARIANNE   What is it then?

MOTHER   I wonder how it would have been had we confided in each other. If we had talked over everything that occurred to us.

MARIANNE   And you never did?

MOTHER   No. We had a rule that our parents taught us: *Each one copes with his own troubles.*

MARIANNE   Do you regret it?

MOTHER   Not regret exactly. I can't say that. But I can't help thinking about our heroic silence. I'm sure it must have tormented him quite a lot. He was such a lively person. Much gayer and more open than I.

MARIANNE *(Moved)*   Do you reproach yourself, Mummy?

MOTHER   I don't know. But it *is* ghastly. No, not ghastly, that's far too dramatic a word. It's extraordinary that two people live a whole life together without . . .

MARIANNE   Without touching each other.

MOTHER   Perhaps that's what I mean.

MARIANNE   And now you think it was your fault?

MOTHER   You mean I'm sitting here with a guilty conscience? No, I'm not. We did our best. All the same . . .

MARIANNE   You can't help thinking of . . .

MOTHER   It sounds so stilted if you put it into words. He has vanished in the darkness and taken his life with him. But the funny thing is that he has taken my life too. *(Smiles)* This is what's called facing the truth, isn't it?

MARIANNE *(Deeply affected)*   You and I have never talked like this before.

MOTHER   We've never had time.

MARIANNE   Or inclination.

MOTHER   I've always been a little scared of you.

MARIANNE *(Smiling)*   Scared? Of me?

MOTHER   You've always been so capable.

MARIANNE   What about yourself?

MOTHER *(Shaking her head)*   If you only knew how anxious I've been about not doing everything perfectly.

MARIANNE *(Touched)*   But you *are* perfect.

MOTHER   Sometimes I'm a little girl of seven, walking in the woods with a father and holding his hand. I'm growing old and sentimental, that's the truth.

MARIANNE   May I ask you something else?

MOTHER *(Smiling)*   It can't be avoided, can it?

MARIANNE   Why were you so furious with me when Johan and I were divorced five years ago? When it was he who got himself another woman and walked out on me?

MOTHER   I wasn't furious at all. I was merely sorry.

MARIANNE   But you criticized me all the time.

MOTHER   I don't remember that.

MARIANNE   It was all my fault.

MOTHER   Did I say that?

MARIANNE   Yes, you did.

MOTHER   I've forgotten.

MARIANNE   I think you might have sided with me that time.

And helped me a little. But you didn't. I wonder why.

MOTHER   I remember just the opposite. I know I said to your father that whatever we did we mustn't interfere and that at all costs we must behave as usual. It was he who was furious, not I.

MARIANNE *(Smiling)* It just goes to show. *(Looking at the time)* Heavens, I must fly. I'm late as it is.

MOTHER   Do you have to go already?

MARIANNE   I'll come again tomorrow. And we can have another talk. I'll be here about five.

MOTHER   Then we can have dinner together.

MARIANNE   I'm afraid I'm asked out to dinner. But I can stay until six thirty.

MOTHER   Can't you bring your dress with you, then you needn't go home and change?

MARIANNE   Yes, I could do that.

MOTHER *(Impulsively)* It was so nice to talk to each other.

MARIANNE *(On her way out)* Let's do it more often.

MOTHER   Do go out to the kitchen and say hello to Miss Alm. She'll be mortally offended if you go without seeing her.

MARIANNE   Heavens, yes! I'll go and say hello to her. So long, Mummy, take care of yourself.

MOTHER   Give my love to Henrik and the children.

MARIANNE   Henrik's away, he won't be home until Saturday.
Bye!

━━━━━

JOHAN *is sitting in his workroom at the institute, busy with some typing. Nowadays he is clean-shaven and wears glasses.* EVA *looks in.*

EVA   Am I disturbing you?

JOHAN   Well . . .

EVA   What are you and your wife doing this evening?

JOHAN   We're busy, as a matter of fact.

EVA *(Smiling)*   What a pity.

JOHAN   Oh?

EVA   I'm throwing a little party and I thought you and your wife might care to look in if you had nothing better to do. There'll only be seven or eight of us.

JOHAN   I'm sorry, it's impossible.

EVA *(Smiling)*   Well, have a nice weekend anyway.

JOHAN   Thanks. Same to you.

EVA   Can't we meet some time?

JOHAN   I'm too busy.

EVA   Are you tired of me?

JOHAN   Why, Eva!

EVA If you want to break it off, then say so properly and don't make excuses.

JOHAN All right then. Let's break it off.

EVA Thank heavens for a straight answer. I had a job getting it out of you.

JOHAN I didn't want to hurt you.

EVA *(Gives a laugh)* No, exactly.

JOHAN If you'll forgive me, I must finish writing this damned report.

EVA *(Cheerfully)* Why, of course, my dear, I won't disturb you. Well, thanks for everything. You were an awfully sweet lover, though a bit absent-minded.

JOHAN *(Smiling)* Thank *you*. You also get good marks.

EVA Is there someone else?

JOHAN To be honest, yes.

EVA Who?

JOHAN I'm not telling you.

EVA Is it anyone I know?

JOHAN Possibly.

EVA Is it Lena?

JOHAN I'm not saying any more.

EVA Then it is Lena.

JOHAN   No, it's not Lena.

EVA   Oh, the girl's pretty if it comes to that. But isn't she a shade too young and flighty for you, my sweet?

JOHAN   It's *not* Lena, I said.

EVA   I don't care anyway. Bye-bye, darling.

JOHAN   So long. All the best.
(EVA *goes out and shuts the door.* ARNE *looks in. He's beginning to put on weight, but youthful*)

ARNE   Hi.

JOHAN   Hi.

ARNE   Have a nice weekend.

JOHAN   Thanks. Same to you.

ARNE   These long weekends with the family are the goddamn end. By the way, I heard you were put on to a survey. Should I congratulate you?

JOHAN   There's not the slightest reason.

ARNE   I suspected as much.

JOHAN   I'll be practically cut off from the institute for two years.

ARNE   What a bore! For you.

JOHAN   Anyway, the whole survey's idiotic. In two years, when it's ready, it will be worthless. It's nothing but a political red herring.

ARNE   Can't you go to Hammarberg and say you don't want to do it?

JOHAN   I've already seen him.

ARNE   Well?

JOHAN   He's a clown. Clown number one of the Swedish civil service. Next thing we know he'll be a member of the government.

ARNE   Yes, but what did he say?

JOHAN   He spoke in ciphers. I didn't know what to make of it. Hardly encouraging.

ARNE   Oh, I see. Well, so long. Have you been to bed with Lena?

JOHAN   To tell you the truth, I haven't.

ARNE   But she turns you on, doesn't she?

JOHAN   What about yourself?

ARNE   Well, yes.

JOHAN   I don't think I'd dare.

ARNE   Have you given up?

JOHAN   Call it what you like.

ARNE   I keep fit, anyway. Exercise, tennis. Swimming. Sun lamp. Watch my weight. So that I needn't feel embarrassed. If it should come to a more intimate presentation, I mean. Bare facts and all that. So long.

JOHAN   So long.
   (ARNE *goes out and shuts the door. Quick footsteps are heard in the corridor.* EVA *flings the door open*)

EVA   I suddenly lost my temper.

JOHAN   So I see.

EVA   I think you're a big shit. Not because you've broken it off with me. I'm not complaining. It was fun while it lasted and we both knew it wasn't for life. But to my mind you're a slob for not saying straight out that you'd had enough. Do you know what's wrong with you? You're so fucking spoiled and priggish that everything bores you. You'll end up by being so bored that you'll be anonymous. In a few years you'll become part of those bookshelves. You're smug and cocky and spoiled. You're bone lazy. You must have others who live for you. Do you remember when you went to the doctor for a check-up and he told you that you had shrunk an inch or two? So there.
   (*Sits down*)

JOHAN   (*Echo*)   So there.

EVA   (*No longer so fierce*)   Why don't you hit back? Why don't you raise Cain? Why do you make yourself out so meek, when you're so pompous and stuck-up?

JOHAN   This is really very interesting.

EVA   The explanation is that you're so pompous that . . . You're so spoiled and priggish that . . .

JOHAN   Well, what?

EVA   I'm fond of you, you silly old thing. That's why I'm bawling you out. And I feel sorry for you somehow.

JOHAN   That's kind of you.

EVA So long. Let me know when you're tired of Lena's melon
breasts and long for my flatter but much more motherly
charms.

JOHAN *(Sighing)* It's not Lena.

EVA She's an efficient secretary, I grant you. And I'm sure
awfully kind. But she's too young for you, Johan. You'll
only come to grief with her.

JOHAN I've told you, it's *not* Lena.

EVA   I have my intuition.

JOHAN   Yes, you have, haven't you?

EVA   And I can see that you're terribly involved.

JOHAN   Maybe I am.

EVA   And it can't be anyone else but Lena. So long.

JOHAN   So long.(EVA *goes out and closes the door.* JOHAN *goes on working. The phone rings and he seizes it*) Hello. Hi! Are you ready now? I'll call for you. Oh, you'd rather not. Well, what about the corner of Karlavägen and Grev Turegatan? Will that do? I'll be there in two minutes. Fine. Bye!

═════

JOHAN *has parked at the street corner. He sits huddled up waiting. After a minute or two* MARIANNE *walks along on the other side of the street. When she catches sight of him she beams and starts to run. She gets in beside him, breathless and smiling. She kisses him quickly on the lips. He starts the car.*

MARIANNE   Been waiting long?

JOHAN   No, I just got here.

MARIANNE   I went to see Mummy.

JOHAN   Oh. How is the old girl?

MARIANNE   I think that . . . Oh, I'll tell you later.

JOHAN   Let's go then.

MARIANNE   Oh, what fun this is! I'm so excited! I went out to the country house yesterday and got it ready. Turned on the heating and the refrigerator and straightened up and got in some food. It was just like old times.

JOHAN   Let's see now, how many years is it since I was there?

MARIANNE   Seven, I think.

JOHAN   And you?

MARIANNE   Well, you see, Henrik doesn't care much for the house. He prefers the real country. So as a matter of fact we usually rent it. Occasionally the girls and I go out there for the weekend, but less and less often. Eva and Karin live their own lives nowadays. It's best that way.

JOHAN   And how's your husband?

MARIANNE   He's overworked, of course. And has high blood pressure, but so does everyone. How is your wife doing?

JOHAN   Oh, all right, I think. She's in Italy on a rest cure.

MARIANNE   Isn't it fantastic that our respective spouses are away at the same time!

JOHAN   It strikes me rather as being slightly indecent.

MARIANNE   But that's just what is so delightful.
   (They arrive at the country house. It hasn't changed much. MA-RIANNE *unlocks the door. They go in)*

JOHAN   It looks much the same.

MARIANNE   A bit dilapidated, that's all. It needs fixing up. But right now we can't afford it, so it will have to wait.

JOHAN   How does it feel?

MARIANNE *(Evasively)*   I don't want to know. It's better that way. You'd better drive the car into the garage so that Gustav doesn't see that we're here. He'd be over like a shot to say hello. And the fat would be in the fire if he saw you.

JOHAN   I'll put the car away later. We're going straight up to the bedroom.

MARIANNE *(With a smile)*   It's ridiculous, but I'm as nervous as if it were the first time.

JOHAN   But as a matter of fact it's not.
(They lie on the big double bed and hold hands, at first without speaking)

MARIANNE   A penny for your thoughts.

JOHAN   I was trying to think whether it was you who seduced me or I who seduced you.

MARIANNE   It was almost a year ago. Yes, it was. The eighth of May, the day before my birthday. Just fancy that. And today's the twenty-eighth of April.

JOHAN   It was you who seduced me.

MARIANNE   Yes, it was.

JOHAN   Did you ever go and see the second act of that play?

MARIANNE   No. It must have looked odd when we sneaked off like two criminals at the intermission.

JOHAN   What decided you?

MARIANNE   I don't know. The second I entered the theater I saw you sitting there all alone. You looked so lonely. So it seemed quite natural to pounce on you at the intermission.

JOHAN   I was awfully pleased, actually.

MARIANNE   And I was pleased that you were pleased.

JOHAN   And you said right off, let's get out of here and go back to my place. My husband's away and won't be home until Friday.

MARIANNE   You blushed.

JOHAN   You bet your sweet life I did. I got such a hard-on that I could hardly stand up straight.

MARIANNE   *(Smiling)*   It was nothing to the way I felt.

JOHAN   We hadn't seen each other for about two years.

MARIANNE   Two years. That's right.

JOHAN   And now we're celebrating our first anniversary.

MARIANNE   No.

JOHAN   What do you mean?

MARIANNE   We're celebrating our twentieth anniversary. We got married in August twenty years ago.

JOHAN   So we did. Twenty years.

MARIANNE   A whole life. We've lived a whole grown-up life with each other. How strange to think of it.
(Weeps suddenly)

JOHAN   *(Gently)*   Dearest. Dearest heart.

MARIANNE   Oh, Johan, isn't it funny? I mean, lying here in this wretched old bed again. It has been different this last year when we've had our hotel rooms. They were suitably impersonal. But this . . .

JOHAN *(Kindly)* Perhaps it was silly of us to come here. Perhaps we should have gone to Denmark instead, as I first suggested.

MARIANNE We didn't have time. And this is quite all right.

JOHAN No, it isn't all right at all. Do you know what I'll do?

MARIANNE I'll soon get used to it.

JOHAN I'll call up Fredrik. He has a cottage not far from here down by the water. You know.

MARIANNE But how can we get in?

JOHAN   There's sure to be a neighbor who has a key. I'm going to phone anyway.

MARIANNE   No, what's the point?

JOHAN   There's no harm in trying. *(Leafs through an address book, dials a number)* Fredrik? Hello, it's Johan. How are you? *(Pause)* Oh, I'm fine. *(Clears his throat)* Look, this is rather a delicate matter. Are you alone? I mean, can we talk freely? Do you think you could lend me your fishing cottage over the weekend? *(Pause)* Hahaha. Yes, right the first time. Though it's not what you think. Hahaha. Very pretty, let me tell you. Young? Well, damn it, she *is* a bit young perhaps. Hahaha. It's all rather tricky, you see. Thanks a lot. I hope I can do you a favor some time. Look, don't say anything to Birgit, will you. She wouldn't understand this sort of thing. Hahaha. You know how women are. Oh, the key's under the step, is it. *(Pause)* Fine. What? Blonde. Nice figure. I'm not saying. Not over the phone. Let's have dinner together one day, eh? I'll call you. Give my love to Birgit. No, better not, at that.(MARIANNE *and* JOHAN *giggle and laugh.* MARIANNE *has taken out a bag with nightgown and toilet things, and a shopping bag with food.)* Come on, let's go. What on earth's in that bag?

MARIANNE   It's only the food we have to take with us, silly. *(They drive off. Arrive at the cottage. It's in a wretched state.* JOHAN *tries to get the fire going.* MARIANNE *goes up to him. Her feelings get the better of her, tears come to her eyes.* JOHAN *turns around)*

JOHAN   What is it? Crying?

MARIANNE   It's so touching. I *am* a fool.

JOHAN   Touching, am I? I'll be damned!

MARIANNE   Yes, you are. Johan, my dearest. You've grown so small in some way.

JOHAN *(Embarrassed)*   Do you too think I've shrunk?

MARIANNE   You're much more handsome than before. And you look so gentle and kind. You always had such a tense look before, sort of anxious and on your guard.

JOHAN   Oh, really?

MARIANNE   Are people beastly to you?

JOHAN *(Smiling)*   I don't really know. I think perhaps I've stopped defending myself. Someone said I'd grown slack and gave in too easily. That I diminished myself. It's not true. If anything, I think I've found my right proportions. And that I've accepted my limitations with a certain humility. That makes me kind and a bit mournful.

MARIANNE *(Tenderly)*   And you with your great expectations.

JOHAN   No, you're wrong. It was my father who had the great expectations, not I. But I wanted so desperately to please Daddy, so I tried all the time to live up to *his* expectations. Not mine. When I was little I had very modest and pleasant ideas as to what I would do when I grew up.

MARIANNE *(Smiling)*   What were they?

JOHAN   Have I never told you?

MARIANNE   If so I've forgotten.

JOHAN   Yes, of course. *(Pause)* Well, you see, I had an old uncle. He had a little store at Sigtuna that sold books and toys and stationery. I was often allowed to go and see him, as I was a sickly child and in need of quiet and fresh air. Sometimes he and Aunt Emma let me help them in the store. I liked that more than anything. My dream was to own a store like that. There you have my ambitions.

MARIANNE   Yes, we should have had a little store. *(Smiles)* How content we'd have been. We'd have grown fat and comfortable and had a lot of children, and slept well and been respected and have joined some local society and never quarreled.

JOHAN   How strange, talking about all that never was. Anyway, you'd never have settled down in some sleepy little place in the country.

MARIANNE   No, that's true. *(Serious)* I used to dream of pleading the cause of the oppressed. There were no limits to my ambitions. And then I became a divorce lawyer. Come on, let's straighten up.

━━━━━━

MARIANNE *and* JOHAN *are sitting at the table. They have eaten, and are sipping wine. A paper lantern is lit.*

MARIANNE   A penny for your thoughts.

JOHAN   It just struck me that you and I have begun telling each other the truth.

MARIANNE   Didn't we before? No, we didn't. Why didn't we? That's odd. Why are we telling the truth now? I know. It's because we make no demands.

JOHAN   We have no secrets from each other.

MARIANNE   Nothing to guard.

JOHAN   In other words, we can tell the truth. After twenty years.

MARIANNE   After twenty years.

JOHAN   Do you think two people who live together day in and day out ever tell the truth to each other? Is it possible, at that?

MARIANNE   It wasn't for us, anyway.

JOHAN   Is it even necessary?

MARIANNE   You mean, suppose that you and I had always told the truth and not kept anything secret from each other?

JOHAN   Did we even know that we kept things secret?

MARIANNE   Of course we lied. I did, anyway.

JOHAN   You! You don't mean it.

MARIANNE   Listen to your tone of voice, Johan.

JOHAN   What goddamn tone of voice?

MARIANNE   The tone of injured innocence. *(Smiles)* At the beginning of our marriage I was unfaithful to you several times. As a matter of fact.

JOHAN   Indeed!

MARIANNE   Are you shocked?

JOHAN   I don't quite know. Yes, I think I am.

MARIANNE   It was all rather harmless. I felt that I was stifling under marriage and childbirth and other duties. So I went in for a spot of adultery.

JOHAN   I'll be damned.

MARIANNE   In pretty quick succession I had three rather cozy little affairs with men you don't know. If you ask me about my conscience, it never said a word.

JOHAN   I see. Well, well. Just goes to show.

MARIANNE   I felt that my affairs were a slight recompense for the suffering I was caused.

JOHAN   If only we'd told the truth.

MARIANNE   If I had told the truth in the spring of nineteen fifty-five, the truth would have pulverized our marriage. I would have broken with our families, sold our two daughters, and killed you. Although in fact I loved you. For I did.

JOHAN   But later?

MARIANNE   Later I got tired.

JOHAN   Of me?

MARIANNE   No, I got tired of my lovers. It wasn't that kind of liberty I longed for after all. So I tried to adjust myself.

JOHAN   And you said nothing.

MARIANNE   What was the use? Anyway, you were working on your doctoral thesis. And you had a stomach ulcer. So we had to tiptoe around to avoid disturbing you.

JOHAN   But all the same!

MARIANNE   All that mattered just then was for you to get your Ph.D. So truth had to take second place. Superficially, the relationship between men and women has changed. But in reality it's the same as a hundred years ago. Ridiculous, isn't it?

JOHAN   But afterwards?

MARIANNE   Oh, we talked. Quite often.

JOHAN   Without any real openness.

MARIANNE   We made do with convenient half-truths. And both of us had studied psychology, so we could explain almost anything. And we couldn't be bothered to have fights. Now and then, when we really lost our tempers, we had a few words, of course.

JOHAN   But we took them back. Afterwards. It would have been carrying things too far to untangle everything.

MARIANNE   So we resorted to lying. Sometimes more, sometimes less, as it suited us.

JOHAN   Do you apply these experiences to your new marriage?

MARIANNE   Why, of course. I lie all the time.

JOHAN   So do I.

MARIANNE   There, you see.

JOHAN   That is to say, my wife isn't interested in the truth. She has arranged the marriage to our mutual convenience.

MARIANNE   Do you love Anna?

JOHAN   This eternal woman's question. I think she's kind, intelligent, pleasant, clean, well-mannered, presentable, and sexually attractive. I like having breakfast with her.

MARIANNE   And she's willing to look after you?

JOHAN   She says she's fond of me. She doesn't care if I'm clever or not. I can be as tired and insufferable as I like. She says it doesn't matter. She says she feels safe with me. She doesn't want anyone else. It's quite beyond me.

MARIANNE   *(Another tone of voice)*   You've had luck with your lottery ticket, Johan!

JOHAN   Then I suppose I shouldn't be unfaithful to her with you.

MARIANNE   Perhaps you love us both.

JOHAN   There you go, all sententious again. I suppose you have to have a gift for feeling love. I don't have that gift.

MARIANNE   First it was your mother who adored you and thought you were a genius. And then the whole succession of women who have behaved in exactly the same way as your mother. Including me. I wonder what it is in you that sabotages all natural maturity. I'm not saying this to be spiteful, but merely because the question never stops puzzling me.

JOHAN   *(Candidly)*   Nowadays I know the cause and it's not particularly encouraging.

MARIANNE   It would be interesting to hear.

JOHAN   *(Gaily)*   Now you shall hear my hideous secret. I'm a middle-aged boy who never wants to grow up.

MARIANNE   I've known that all along.

JOHAN   I have found it very hard to grasp that I'm a child with genitals. A fabulous combination when it comes to women with maternal feelings.

MARIANNE   Heavens, how banal! I thought at least you were going to confess to some criminal tendencies.

JOHAN *(Continuing)*   And for that reason I never grew up. Why should I? It would mean that I was forced to manage on my own. I might even have to accept responsibility.

MARIANNE   What an awful anticlimax, Johan dear.

JOHAN   I don't *want* to mature, you see. That's why Anna is a good wife.

MARIANNE   Poor Anna.

JOHAN *(Smiling)*   Your sympathy doesn't ring true. Now let's talk about you instead.

MARIANNE *(Laughing)*   Weren't we going to have dinner?

———

They have now had dinner and have settled down comfortably in front of the fire. It is dusk. They are sitting in easy chairs and smoking in silence

MARIANNE   You want to know how I get along with Henrik, my husband?

JOHAN   Not any more.

MARIANNE   It was silly of us to get married at all. Or shall I say it was rash? We looked on it more or less as a joke. Two people can live together year in and year out without being married and it's quite a different matter from living together when they *are* married.

JOHAN   When did you meet?

MARIANNE   Oh, some years ago. If you'll forgive my saying so, it was a purely sexual affair.

JOHAN   Oh. Oh, I see.

MARIANNE   Henrik is very, how shall I put it, convincing on that point. *(Smiles)* Sex really turns him on and he persuaded me that I was just as avid as he was. As you know, I wasn't all that hot for it in the old days.

JOHAN   So I remember.

MARIANNE   You don't like my talking about this?

JOHAN   No, I don't. But it can't be helped.

MARIANNE   Frankly, I was obsessed by this new thing that I had never known. I found I was insatiable. *(Smiles)* It sounds crazy.

JOHAN   I think it sounds nice. For you, I mean.

MARIANNE   As you can imagine, I fell hard for Henrik and couldn't do without him. He was also pretty crazy about me. But I soon found out that he was having other women on the side.

JOHAN   Well I never!

MARIANNE   At first I was terribly hurt and humiliated. I even became jealous.

JOHAN   *You* did?

MARIANNE   We had a violent quarrel. That is to say, *I* was the violent one. I told him to go to hell.

JOHAN   And did he?

MARIANNE   He said I was overwrought. And walked out. After a week or two I begged him on my knees to come back. On *any* conditions. He too thought it was time to resume. We went off on a vacation together. We were very happy. On our return we got married. Since then it has been up and down. Mostly down.

JOHAN   I'm sorry.

MARIANNE   Henrik is an overwhelmingly active person. He's senior physician at the General Hospital. He's also on dozens of committees and on top of that spends every spare minute doing research. I just don't know how he does it.

JOHAN   Especially if he has a private practice with a lot of ladies at the same time.

MARIANNE   His health isn't too good. He has high blood pressure and has to keep taking medicine. Sometimes I feel I can't stand him another minute. That he'll be the death of me with all his demands.

JOHAN   That's not very nice for someone with your insistence on liberty, is it?

MARIANNE   Oddly enough it's just the reverse.

JOHAN   I don't get you.

MARIANNE   Today I'm no longer dependent on him. I live with him. That's fine. I live with you. That's fine. If I meet some other man who attracts me I can live with him too.

JOHAN   Do you call *that* liberty?

MARIANNE   For the time being it's liberty.

JOHAN   And you're happy?

MARIANNE   Sometimes I'm extremely unhappy when by rights I should be happy, and just the opposite. The feeling of happiness follows no rules. At least not with me.

JOHAN   There's something I'd like to ask you.

MARIANNE   *(With a nod)*   You want to know if I'm still in the habit of getting my own back on the sexual plane. *(Laughs)* I tried all right. But he never paid any attention. He merely said I bored him with that sort of nonsense. And devoted himself to some other woman with the same all-absorbing interest. And there I was, high and dry with my revenge. So I've stopped all that. You and I also have it good nowadays. Don't we, Johan my darling?

JOHAN   Yes, of course.

MARIANNE   Are you jealous?

JOHAN   I feel both attracted and repelled.

MARIANNE   Do you remember what we had drummed into us as children? All that rubbish about physical love being the most sacred and beautiful thing there was? That the body was a temple and that you mustn't cheapen yourself. Or something equally idiotic. To make love to someone was almost a sacrament. Everything was so precious and delicate and wonderful that we got the jitters when we tried to put it into practice. At the other extreme was pornography, with lurid descriptions of the sex act and colossal feats of incessant orgasm. That was also pretty depressing. *(Pause)* What's up, Johan? You look so thoughtful.

JOHAN   *(Smiling suddenly)*   I was thinking that everything's fine. Just fine. Tremendously good. Couldn't be better. It's just that I can't stand it.

MARIANNE   I knew you didn't want to hear the truth.

JOHAN *(Fiercely)*   Do you think I care about your orgasms with that goddamn slob and his blood pressure? You're welcome to them. I'm full of admiration for your complete emancipation. It's most impressive. You should damn well write a novel. I bet you'd be applauded by Women's Lib.

MARIANNE   You can't mean to be as stupid as you sound.

JOHAN   I tell you I couldn't care less about it all.

MARIANNE   But it suddenly mattered so terribly.

JOHAN   No, not really. It's just a little bit of all the marvelous things life has to offer. Think of all our knowledge! Think of all the wisdom and awareness that we've arrived at through tears and misery. It's magnificent. Fantastic. We've discovered ourselves. It's out of this world. One perceives his smallness. The other her greatness. Could it be better? Here we sit so sensibly, talking rubbish about our better halves. They're almost with us in the room. We wave to them. It's mental group sex on the top level. It might all be taken from a textbook on lifemanship. It's unheard-of, Marianne. Analysis is total, knowledge is boundless. But I can't stand it.

MARIANNE *(Sad suddenly)*   I know what you mean.

JOHAN   Do you really?

MARIANNE *(Sadly)*   I know what you mean, but I don't think it's so terrible.

JOHAN   Hmm, that's the big difference between you and me. Because I refuse to accept the complete meaninglessness behind the complete awareness. I can't live with that cold light over all my endeavors. If you only knew how I struggle with my meaninglessness. Over and over again I try to cheer myself up by saying that life has the value that you yourself ascribe to it. But that sort of talk is no help to me. I want something to long for. I want something to believe in.

MARIANNE   I don't feel as you do.

JOHAN   No, I realize that.

MARIANNE   Unlike you, I stick it out. And enjoy it. I rely on my common sense. And my feeling. They cooperate. I'm satisfied with both of them. Now that I'm older I have a third coworker: my experience.

JOHAN   *(Gruff)*   You should be a politician.

MARIANNE   *(Serious)*   Maybe you're right.

JOHAN   Good Lord!

MARIANNE   I like people. I like negotiations, prudence, compromises.

JOHAN   You're practicing your election speech, I can hear it.

MARIANNE   You think I'm difficult.

JOHAN   Only when you preach.

MARIANNE   I won't say another word.

JOHAN   Promise not to tell me any more homely truths this evening?

MARIANNE   I promise.

JOHAN   Promise not to harp on that orgasm athlete?

MARIANNE   Not another word about him.

JOHAN   Do you think that *for just a little while* you can restrain your horrible sententiousness?

MARIANNE   It will be difficult, but I'll try.

JOHAN   Can you possibly, I say *possibly*, ration your boundless female strength?

MARIANNE   I see that I'll have to.

JOHAN   Come on then. Let's go to bed.

———

During the night MARIANNE *wakes up and screams with horror.* JOHAN *puts on the light and tries to put his arms around her to calm her, but she breaks loose, leaps up, and starts pacing to and fro.* JOHAN *waits in silence for her to say something.*

MARIANNE   I can't think why it is I dream like that. What do you think causes it?

JOHAN   Perhaps you ate something that didn't agree with you.

MARIANNE   Do you think so?

JOHAN   Or else, dearest Marianne, in your extremely well-ordered world there is something you can't get at.

MARIANNE   What would that be?

JOHAN   How should I know?

MARIANNE   Put your arms around me. I'm shivering so terribly. Although I'm so hot. Do you think I'm catching something? The children have just had colds.

JOHAN *(Gently)* There, there. You'll soon feel better.

MARIANNE Pull the blanket up over my shoulders, will you? Like that, that's lovely. Now I feel much better.

JOHAN Don't you remember what frightened you?

MARIANNE We have to go along a dangerous road or something. I want you others to take my hands so that we can hold on to each other. *(Frightened)* But it's no good. I no longer have any hands. I only have a couple of stumps that end at the elbows. At that moment I am slithering in soft sand. I can't get hold of you. You're all standing up there on the road and I can't reach you.

JOHAN *(Tenderly)*   What a horrible dream.

MARIANNE *(After a pause)*   Johan!

JOHAN   Yes, my dear.

MARIANNE   Do you think we're living in utter confusion?

JOHAN   You and I?

MARIANNE   No, the whole lot of us.

JOHAN   What do you mean by confusion?

MARIANNE   Fear, uncertainty, folly. I mean confusion. That we realize secretly that we're slipping downhill. And that we don't know what to do.

JOHAN   Yes, I think so.

MARIANNE   Perhaps it's like a poison.

JOHAN   Inside us, you mean?

MARIANNE   Just think if everything really is too late.

JOHAN   We mustn't say things like that. Only think them.

MARIANNE   Think how we exert ourselves all the time.

JOHAN   Especially you.

MARIANNE   Johan . . .

JOHAN   Yes?

MARIANNE   Have we missed something important?

JOHAN   All of us?

MARIANNE   You and I.

JOHAN   What would that be?

MARIANNE   Sometimes I know exactly how you're feeling and thinking. And then I feel a great tenderness for you and forget about myself, even though I don't efface myself. Do you understand what I mean?

JOHAN   I understand what you mean.

MARIANNE   Sometimes I can identify myself with a complete stranger too, and understand him. Those are brief moments of insight.

JOHAN   If we were to trust in that sort of sentimental fellow-feeling, nothing would ever get done, I can assure you.

MARIANNE   Johan.

JOHAN   Yes?

MARIANNE   Sometimes it grieves me that I have never loved anyone. I don't think I've ever been loved either. It really distresses me.

JOHAN   I think you're too tense about this.

MARIANNE   *(Smiling)*   Do you?

JOHAN   I can only answer for myself. And I think I love you in my imperfect and rather selfish way. And at times I think you love me in your stormy, emotional way. In fact, I think that you and I love one another. In an earthly and imperfect way.

MARIANNE   Do you really think so?

JOHAN   You're so damned hard to please.

MARIANNE   Yes, I am.

JOHAN   But here I sit with my arms around you, without any fuss, in the middle of the night in a dark house, somewhere in the world. And your arms are around me. I can't honestly say I have any great insight or fellow-feeling.

MARIANNE   No, you haven't.

JOHAN   Presumably I don't have the imagination for that.

MARIANNE   No, you're rather unimaginative.

JOHAN   I don't know what the hell my love looks like. I can't describe it and I hardly ever feel it in everyday life.

MARIANNE   And you think I love you too?

JOHAN   Yes, perhaps you do. But if we harp on it too much, love will give out.

MARIANNE   We're going to sit like this all night.

JOHAN   Oh no, we're not!

MARIANNE   Why not?

JOHAN   One leg has gone to sleep and my left arm is practically dislocated. I'm very sleepy and my back's cold.

MARIANNE   Well then, let's snuggle down.

JOHAN   Yes, let's.

MARIANNE   Good night, my darling. And thanks for the talk.

JOHAN   Good night.

MARIANNE   Sleep well.

JOHAN   Thanks, the same to you.

MARIANNE   Good night.